PREVENTING
A
CHURCH
SPLIT

CHRISTIAN BOOKS
AUBURN, MAINE

PREVENTING
A
CHURCH
SPLIT

by Gene Edwards
and
Tom Brandon

Published by Christian Books
Publishing House
P.O. Box 3368
Auburn, Maine 04210

CONTENTS

PART TWO
by Tom Brandon

DEDICATION

To every minister who, when faced with the possibility of a church split—no matter how unfair it might be, refuses to fight. To every Christian who, no matter how unsatisfactory the situation in the church might be, refuses to become part of a complaining faction.

To all believers who—when facing a church split—choose, rather, a crucifixion.

A WORD OF THANKS

After completing this manuscript I asked a Christian lawyer and a good friend named Tom Brandon to add a section to this book. When you read what he has written you will understand why I asked him to add his insights to this book. Tom has formerly served full time with Christian Legal Society and is presently in a full time ministry of reconciliation. I wish to recommend Tom's ministry to all who read this book, feeling sure that the day will come in many of your lives that his help will be needed and appreciated. He can be contacted by writing or calling Thomas S. Brandon, Box 331142, Fort Worth, Texas 76133.

And one more expression of gratitude. Once again, thank you, Ann Witkower, for doing the editing on this book too. Without you there would be no books.

CHAPTER 1

CHURCH SPLITS
I HAVE KNOWN

I was nine years old when I witnessed my first church split. My family lived in Bay City, Texas at that time. I am going to tell you the story of that split, and others I have witnessed. You need to hear these stories, because they could save your life.

As soon as we moved to Bay City my mother became one of the "faithful" at the only Southern Baptist Church in town. She loved that church, and went to all the meetings just like all devout Baptists. I still have vivid memories, for instance, of how she and a few other people in the church secretly raised money to surprise the pastor with a new car on his birthday. Like so many others in the church, my mother thought highly of the pastor. Unfortunately, that opinion was not unanimous.

Seared in my mind forever is the scene of a Wednesday night business session. All I knew was there was some sort of dispute, and Christians were going at one another tongue and lip. My mother, Gladys by name, tried to stand and say something but instead managed only to break into tears. That night, before the eyes of a nine year old kid, the church split. Over what I do not know. I only know that the pastor left. Shortly thereafter another church was formed.

As a result of this highly emotional and physically debilitating split, Mom led her two boys over to the First Christian Church, there to continue the family's religious life. I would probably have grown up to be a Christian instead of a Baptist (pun intended) except that soon after landing at the Christian church, it had a fight!

My mother never recovered. (She stopped going to church entirely, though she never stopped loving her Lord.) In fact, she had a complete emotional breakdown. A total emotional collapse, by the way, is not an unusual result for someone to experience as a result of a church split. *Mark that fact.*

Nor was Gladys the only person profoundly affected by that split. A generation later when no one in Bay City even knew that the visiting minister speaking in their city, whose name was Gene Edwards, had ever lived there, it was my observation that the pain, damage and memory of that split was still very much alive in Bay City.

Nothing compares to church division in its power to cause Christians to stop following the Lord. Sin, temptation, adultery, divorce, illness—all pale in the presence of the power of division. It is my studied judgment that more Christians have walked away from the things of God because of church splits than for any other reason.

A short time after these two church crises in Bay City, it happened that my dad was transferred to a new oilfield company located in the dusty little sawmill town of Cleveland, Texas. As all good Southern Baptists do, I moved my "letter" to the local Baptist church there. I had no more than sat down in the pew when that church had a fight! Right there in the Sunday morning worship service, no less.

(The scene: the pastor offered his resignation and then made the mistake of adding a few words. He had been physically accosted by one of the deacons on the Wednesday night previous. Just when he was about to refer to that incident someone out in the pews jumped up and started screaming at him.)

I was thirteen years old. That was my third church split in four years. For the next two years I lived a "split-free" life. How lucky can you get. Then, at age fifteen, I entered college. I arrived at the college town of Commerce, Texas just after the First Baptist Church there threw out their pastor.

Well, a year and a half later, the day before my seventeenth birthday, I was converted to Jesus Christ. Yes, sometimes you become a Baptist, then you get saved! At about that same time Dr. Elmer Page became the church's new pastor. I have to tell you right off that this man meant a lot to me as a new Christian and later as a young minister.

In coming to Commerce to become pastor of the largest church in this university town, Dr. Page did not know he was walking into a hornet's nest. Before Dr. Page was called to this church, the deacons had been divided as to which of two men should be their new pastor. One faction had finally prevailed and Dr. Page was called. A catastrophic fight was inevitable.

It is always difficult to understand the many ingredients which go into a church battle. Who can trace the complex roots and fiber of a community, its past conflicts, animosities, cliques, feuds, and unhealed wounds of yesteryear? We all look so beautiful when we come together on Sunday, dressed up in suits and smiles. None of those undercurrents show. But they are there.

No, we can't understand all the ingredients of a church split, but one night I sat at ringside and watched that particular church blow wide open. I was supposed to be the main speaker that night. As it turned out, I was lucky to be able to read one

Scripture verse. The fight was the whole show. The story goes like this.

As a student at the nearby university, I belonged to a group of Christian college kids who loved the Lord, and one another, very much. We had gone through a lot together, and together had experienced some remarkable times with the Lord. Being college students, we knew nothing of the internal struggle going on in the church.

Paradoxically, the church was seeing incredible evangelistic results during the very time this smoldering conflict was going on. Hundreds of people were being brought to the Lord. Nonetheless, Dr. Page was under enormous pressure to resign. The "other group" still wanted that other man to be their pastor. (Sadly, the other preacher was helping things along!)

It was right in the middle of this grit and glory that God called me to the ministry. A few days later I graduated and set off for the seminary. And just a few days after that Dr. Page asked me to preach on the following Sunday night. I accepted. After all, the invitation sounded innocent enough. Besides, I was eighteen years old, had been a preacher and seminary student only a few days, and it was an invitation to speak at "First Church." *Of course I accepted!* What I did not know was that I was about to be thrown to the lions. You see, the next Sunday morning Dr. Page stunned everyone. He resigned. That left me the speaker in the evening service of a now pastorless church. What followed that evening is really quite impossible to describe or believe.

I stepped out of my car that evening, walked around to the back of the church building, and opened the door to the choir's dressing room. The "youth choir" was going to sing that evening, so the room was filled with my college friends. Everyone was excited because one of their very own was going to preach that night. The choir director, on the other hand, stood in stunned silence like a man who had seen a room full of ghosts. He had. He had just opened the door and peeked out at the congregation. There were deacons sitting out there in the audience who had not been inside that church in a decade. There were members of the church present who had not attended a meeting in twenty-five years.

The music began. The choir filed out. I followed and took my place near the pulpit. The sight that greeted my eyes was incomprehensible. The building was packed. The balcony, which was usually never used, was full. It was the largest number of people I had ever seen in that church on Sunday evening. For one short instant this young dumb kid thought they had all come to hear him preach.

Need I tell you? They hadn't.

My brother had come to hear me speak that night. A devout Christian lady had managed to get her unsaved husband inside the church for the first time ever because I was speaking. Some few others had probably come to hear me speak, but for the life of me I could not figure out who all the other people were.

The service commenced with singing and then a prayer. The time arrived for the evening message. Just as I was about to walk to the pulpit, someone in the audience stood and said, "I make a motion that we go into a church business meeting." Instantly came, "Second the motion."

Not until the next day was I to know exactly what had happened to bring about this phenomenal scene. It seems that just after the Sunday morning service the disenfranchised deacons spent the entire day on the phone calling everyone on the church roll who could be counted on to vote on their side. That massive throng had assembled for one purpose: to regain control of the church.

What happened next lived as a nightmare in the minds of hundreds of believers for years to come. For over two hours, a clash of tongues and wills continued. It was brutal. Even now my pen shakes as I recall that horrifying evening. It was brother against brother, sister against sister. Finally, a vote was taken;

the "outs" got back in. The instant the vote was counted dozens of people began filing out the door. Their task was complete.

What did I do that night? I walked to the pulpit, opened my Bible and read these words — "Except you repent you shall all perish" — and dismissed the meeting.

You might say that was my introduction to the Christian ministry.

(After the meeting a visiting missionary in the audience came over to me and said, "Gene, if you use that much wisdom in your ministry for all the rest of your life, you will truly be a wise man." The words were wasted. I have never once since that night ever had that much wisdom!)

Just a few days ago I was in Texas at a reunion of those wonderful Christian kids I had gone through college with.* We have managed to stay in contact with one another for over a generation. Even at the reunion, *thirty-six years later,* that awful night was remembered and the pain relived. Think of that. Thirty-six years and the pain was still there. It is a memory we cannot get past. We plan to meet again when we all turn seventy. Even then we will remember that night and shutter.

You can only imagine what it was like in the days immediately after the fight. The name of the Lord was disgraced in the entire community. Several people became physically ill. At least one from our group was sick for nearly a year. Christians became embittered. The church, of course, was rent to shreds.

But this is the fact you must be impressed with: That night at the First Baptist Church in Commerce, Texas many Christians in the audience were seeing their third, or fourth, or *fifth* church split. Know this, *most Christians can only take just so many church splits before bailing out of the church entirely.* Some Christians can survive one split. A few can survive two. A

---

*See the introduction to *The Inward Journey.*

handful of steel-coated souls may survive three. That is about the limit of human endurance. That is a hard, cold fact. Keep that fact in mind on the day you are about to start, or join, your first church fight.

You may survive a church split you join, especially if it is your first. But many others in your group will not survive, because it will not be their first time. For many, that split will be their *last!* Later on, as you grow older, it will be your turn. You will be seeing your second or third church fight. And somewhere around three or four, no matter who you are, you will reach the end of your ability to survive spiritually.

I ask you, dear reader, is anything you believe or think, any doctrine, any opinion you hold, worth such carnage? In every church fight there are those going down for the third time. Do you want to play a role in the destruction of a believer's life?

There is a verse in Acts that says, "They cursed the name of God because of you." There are Christians, and non-Christians, who walk out of church buildings and at that moment give up all pretense of being Christian (or of becoming a Christian) because of the ways of Christians. Unfortunately, it happened that night in Commerce, Texas long ago. It has happened thousands upon thousands of times in hundreds of thousands of churches across our land. It will happen again tomorrow, somewhere.

Someday you are going to be in a meeting like the one I was in, there in east Texas. It takes a certain kind of bravery to foment a split, join a split, or fight those who are splitting. But it is a bravery we don't need, for it is a bravery born of *the fall of man!*

Stay away from splits. They are a kind of spiritual madness.

And if you think church fights are rare, remember this. I was eighteen years old that night in Commerce, Texas. I had been a Christian less than two years, yet I had witnessed *four church fights* in *nine* years.

7

My best calculations are that about five percent of all Protestant churches split every year. That would mean about fifteen thousand splits per year in America alone. The dead ones seem to split the least, so some have to split frequently to keep the statistics up.

One of the most difficult things for a new Christian to comprehend is that Christians split, fight, war, and ruthlessly immolate one another. Not believing this gruesome fact can destroy you. Believe it. The chances of your being in a hideous church fight, soon, stands at about *100%*.

Three years after I entered the seminary I was called to be pastor of a Baptist church. Three years later I was called to another pastorate where I remained for two years. Can you believe it, I managed to go all five of those years without seeing a church split?

(I am, in fact, one of the most fortunate of ministers. I have personally seen only one division in my ministry.)

At the end of my second pastorate, at the age of twenty-six, I became a Southern Baptist evangelist. Ah, that is the life! You arrive at a church on Sunday morning, preach evangelistic sermons for a week, and leave the next Sunday (by air), totally unscratched. In fact, you usually depart as somewhat of a hero. In fact I do not recall making a single enemy in all the years I was an evangelist. I led a charmed life. But the pastors I worked with, that was a different story.

During those years as an evangelist my eyes were opened to this grisly fact: What I had seen going on in a few Baptist churches as a youth in Texas was taking place all over America, in every evangelical denomination and every organization across the land. Splits and fights were not a local phenomenon; in fact, they were an *international* plague.

Here are a few things I learned as a young evangelist whose ministry went almost everywhere: (1) Churches in general are as dead as a one-hundred-year-old coffin. (2) Most churches are either about to go into a fight, or they are in one, or they are just coming out of one. (3) The practice of the pastoral concept is just about the most nerve-wracking, unnatural, unfair, scripturally unjustifiable invention ever palmed off on the human race.

The *fourth* thing I learned came a little slower, because it is a bit more hidden: Christendom is filled with ministers, pastors, Christian workers, elders, deacons (and other assorted laymen) who are bleeding to death spiritually because of dissension, splits, and fights which they have gone through. Furthermore, this is not a phenomenon relegated to churches, but is just as prevalent in the interdenominational Christian organizations. There is little difference in being "on staff" in an interdenominational organization and being a member of a church. Fights and splits abound in them all.

Why is it that the kingdom of God stands utterly silent in the presence of this carnage? Be clear, I am not speaking here of the big denominational splits that you read about in church history. I am speaking of knockdowns and dragouts in local gatherings.

Splits and divisiveness are the heartbreak of God's people everywhere across this land and across this planet; yet it appears that Christendom has refused even to admit to it. We are knee deep in this nightmarish problem, yet we speak and act as though the problem did not exist. Why, pray tell, do we ignore this worldwide malady?

Back when I was a young pastor, I often went out into the community visiting people, door to door. How many homes have I walked into where I have listened to people tell me they would never darken the door of a church building again as long as they lived. Why? Because of bitter memories of conflicts with other Christians or—more likely—because of church fights. Later, as an evangelist, I was to discover this tale of woe was being told by Christians in neighborhoods all over the Christian world. Such people are out there by the untold millions.

There came a day in my life when I laid down not only the pastoral role but the role of the evangelist. I departed the more traditional expression of the church and walked out into that far smaller world of Christians who meet in homes, who meet informally, who follow no set rituals, and who rarely, if ever, give a name to their gatherings. It is a very small world indeed, where believers belong to no movement or denomination, set up no doctrinal barriers between one another, and where there are no lines distinguishing clergy from laymen.

Frankly, I love it out here in this informal expression of the church, but I surely don't recommend it. Stay in the more traditional church if that is where you are now.

Why? Well, how many people are there in the traditional Protestant and evangelical churches? Somewhere between twenty and sixty million in North America? But how many people are in those nameless little groups out there meeting in homes? Nobody knows. Ten thousand? Fifty thousand? Five thousand? Whatever the number of simple believers meeting out there in homes, you can be sure they are few in number; they are also very serious about their Christian commitment. Believers meeting in homes are not only committed to the Lord and to His church, but they are also very involved in one another's lives. This commitment and involvement is both wonderful and hazardous. Sad to say, there is as much division among believers outside the institutional churches as there is within them. And when division comes to us out here, because the bonds are so close the pain is even deeper.

So when I speak of a worldwide problem, I speak of every level of Christendom from cathedrals to home meetings. Whether you belong to a more traditional church or a wholly informal church, there is just too much division in churches. Can this situation be changed? *That* is the hope behind this book.

CHAPTER 2

JUST HOW BAD ARE CHURCH SPLITS?

Last week I was at a conference in a southern city of America. I would like to tell you two stories that came to my attention just *last week*. They are included only because they happened so recently.

A group of twenty-five believers had just begun meeting and were having a wonderful time when, after only five or six meetings, they split. I observed to one of the people involved, "You are so fortunate it happened now." In tears she asked, "Why, when it is so painful and so damaging?" My reply was, "But the pain now is nothing to compare to a division that might have come a few years from now, when bonds of love and interlocking friendships would have been deeply established. Then you would be seeing divorce, nervous breakdowns, perhaps even people having to be sedated, and others under psychiatric care. A worst case scenario may even see someone temporarily committed to a sanitarium. *It gets that bad."*

A man sitting at the table with me, who had been through two or three such holocausts, uttered a very quiet "Amen."

Yes, it gets *that* bad.

That same day, at the same conference, a young man recounted to me the story of a church he had been a member of since its beginning. There was great growth, a split, hundreds damaged, his father and mother divorced. The church recovered, split again, recovered, split again; finally he and his wife divorced. Recently, he told me, he had been asked by the church not to participate in any leadership role and, most interesting of all, the church is now the size it was when it began, about thirty-five people at the end of ten years.

Yes, it gets *that* bad. Laymen are destroyed. Ministers are destroyed. Men's and women's lives are wrecked for as long as they live on this planet.

This is how bad a church split is. Are you sure you want to be part of one?

CHAPTER 3

CHURCH SPLITS DON'T HAPPEN TO NICE PEOPLE

Have you ever wondered what preachers talk about when they are alone with one another? The Bible? Prayer? God? Nope! More likely they are discussing things you have never heard preached, or even mentioned.

When I became a student of theology at Southwestern Baptist Seminary, one of the most interesting things I noticed was the main topic of conversation in the cafeteria. It was not the Lord or evangelism or missions, or our terribly profound seminary studies. Nor was it the wonderful things you hear us talking about in the pulpit on Sunday morning. Those young preachers talked about the gargantuan problems and pressures they were facing in their churches: discord, hurt feelings, fights, bickering, and the spectre of a looming split.

A little later, when I became one of those young pastors, I regularly attended a weekly meeting of about thirty Baptist

13

pastors serving churches in the area. The number one topic, as we talked to one another informally, was major church problems—"those a'comin' and them a'goin'."

Today, if I were to sit down in a restaurant with a group of fellow ministers—and if we were all alone, no "laymen" present—we would probably end up discussing the tremendous, horrendous experiences that drain our lives, destroy our fellow workers, and devastate "lay" Christians.

I speak not just for ministers whom I know. This is the number one concern of the overwhelming majority of pastors on this planet. Nor does it end with ministers. This pain is being carried about in the hearts and memories of literally millions of Christians.

If you listen to a group of ministers at a great conference next week, you will hear them hold forth in spellbinding sermons about Jacob, or Abraham, or Moses, or David, and you will be enthralled with the deep spiritual insight of those speaking. But if, perchance, you see those same speakers in a restaurant together, and if you wonder what they are talking about, they are probably over there quietly bleeding to death because of the horrible schisms and conflicts in the kingdom of God and, more specifically, in their local areas.

Ministers live a dichotomy, speaking on one thing and rarely making mention of the church dissension, splits, and damaged lives; yet these are the weights that rest heaviest on their hearts. Furthermore, this problem, real and everpresent, will touch the life of virtually every Christian, not just ministers.

Do you know an older Christian who has walked with the Lord many years, one who has been through fire, who has known the cross? What does he speak of in private, among his peers? Ask! Most will share with you some hidden pains, or recount stories about Christians' mistreatment of other Christians. The stories, if you dare listen, will sear your ears. Regardless of what flavor of Christian one may be, if a believer

14

has been engaged in the Lord's work for twenty or thirty years, these are the worst and harshest memories of his life.

But why tell you this, dear reader?

The reason is simple. Because the day will come when you will be in the wrong place at the wrong time, and you will be one of those Christians caught in the vortex of a church split. Right now there is a good chance you are just in front of, or in the midst of, or coming out of, a split.

The day will come, if you live long enough, that you will be in a church fight. And if a second one comes, or a third, or—God forbid—a fourth, then your chances of spiritual survival are *nil!* Other than the death of your husband or wife, a church fight could well be the most devastating experience you will ever know.

Perhaps the greatest mistake you can make is to think it will not happen to you or to your church. True, Christendom does not want to talk about this problem. You will hear no sermons preached on the subject, nor instructions given on how to survive. Probably no one will help prepare you to face the very real possibility of a split. You will not be informed of the vastness of devastation a church fight produces in the lives of those involved. But all of that ignorance will not make you immune to the damage found in a church split. It will still come. To *you.*

I suggest we stand up and declare, "This hidden tragedy must be brought out in the open and addressed." Why? Because it will surely fall into your life and the life of every earnest believer.

Frankly, the only sane, fair, proper time to get this monster into the light in your church is when there is no division going on. The church of God desperately needs to practice *preventive maintenance* on the problem of church splits. Right in the middle of a fight is not the best time to address the issue.

15

I plan to practice what I am saying. The day this book comes off the press, I intend to pass it out to every Christian I meet with. And, yes, we have a strong unity among us, and peace prevails. *That* is the best time to face the issue of church division.

But who would want to hear about a church split when there isn't one going on? Absolutely nobody. Not you. Not me. Not anyone. "If we say it's not there it will go away" is the prevailing attitude of Christians toward division and its ensuing carnage.

Furthermore, everyone knows "splits never happen to nice people." My only conclusion is, there must not be any nice people on this earth. I cannot call the name of one human being who is a truly devout Christian and has been one for thirty years who has not witnessed at least one horrendous split. Yet we all seem determined not to admit we have ever even heard of one!

Well, dear reader, church splits don't happen to atheists. They happen to Christians, almost all of them! And dealing with the problem before it happens is merely an evidence of sanity.

I close with an almost humorous story. You know that conference I was in last week? Among those present were the members of a tiny church fellowship just beginning to meet. During a question and answer period I remarked that it is important to face the reality of a church sundering. Two people in this group were immediately provoked. "A church split is not inevitable." "We don't have to have a split." "We *will not* have a church split. We have very wise people among us to prevent such things."

Pride goes before a fall. In less than forty-eight hours, that fellowship of believers split.

Of course your church has people who are even more special than these were? And Napoleon Bonaparte is still living in France!

CHAPTER 4

THE ULTIMATE DANGER

I do not want to write this chapter. And you do not want to read it, or believe it. But what I am about to speak of is true, and if we are to see an end to church splits we have to face the issue raised in this chapter. The issue? In a church split there is always the possibility of physical violence. If that seems a bit farfetched, then you have not read the letters I have read, nor heard the stories I have had to listen to.

To illustrate what I am speaking of, let us look for a moment at a mob. Sociologists tell us there are certain forces, common to any audience, which can produce mob violence. How is it that a collective audience of people can be turned into a crowd, and a crowd into a riot? We are told that political revolutionaries study and then use these very forces in order to incite mob violence.

There are a few simple, invariable facts about human beings. For instance, in every group of any one hundred individuals there are approximately ten people who are naturally hostile to authority; there are also, on an average, five people in that group of one hundred people who become highly emotional under pressure; in this same group there are about four people who, when aroused to hate, become psychologically unstable. It is these four people who may become physically violent if their stress level, or their emotional level, reaches a certain threshold.

Men schooled in inciting mob violence have brought down governments by creating a situation where these three types of people lose their stability in the presence of a harangue. That last group (the four people who are latently violent) will become violent if the situation in an audience heats up enough. Perhaps one of them will attack a policeman. Then four or five other people become hysterical; the authorities move in. Now some of those ten hostile people react hostilely toward the police. Mass hysteria soon takes over, dozens of people are injured, sometimes people are killed, and sometimes governments topple. Professional insurrectionists depend on those who are latently violent, those who are emotionally unstable and those who are naturally hostile to authority to do something violent under pressure.

What in heaven's name does this have to do with Christians? Remember, these statistics more or less hold true in every group of about a hundred people. Yes, even in a church.

Let a preacher stand in front of a people and consistently attack a man, or a group, or a teaching. Out there in the audience is someone who is internalizing all this on a level most of us do not understand. Give that person a steady diet of hate—hate of anything—and he will begin fantasizing about "the enemy." He cracks.

But this works the other way around as well. If someone in the congregation is busy criticizing a minister, someone else is just as apt to crack. It works both ways.

In an atmosphere of criticism, rumor, charge and counter-charge, there is an outside chance that a perfectly normal-looking man might slip a knife into his pocket and carry it around everywhere he goes. If you ask him why, he cannot tell you. Let time pass and let the hate atmosphere continue, and there is a remote possibility he will do something violent. There is even a chance he might make an attempt on someone's life. The more intense the leader's words and the more intense the group's reaction to his words, the greater the chance someone out there is going to act violently.

You don't believe?

Then read my mail.

Or perhaps you think this only happens among fringe groups, and you, after all, are in "mainstream" Christianity. The letters I receive tell me that these things happen more in "mainstream" Christianity than anywhere else.

And keep this in mind, too. Sociology tells us that fanaticism is found almost exclusively in only two areas—politics and religion.

Some examples? A teacher on a highly respected Christian college campus hears a story about a group of Christians meeting in a home in a nearby city. On the basis of erroneous and unverified rumor he labels these dear believers "a fringe group." Rumors escalate. An entire college student body becomes paranoid. An atmosphere of hysteria ensues; someone on the campus reacts violently. The church is actually physically attacked. Evangelicals attacking evangelicals, if you please.

On the other end of the spectrum, a group of men who are the leaders of a national denomination become so consumed with their own rhetoric that they actually gather one night to discuss assassinating a man they hate. Why? Because he is minister in a nearby church and has committed the sin of having his church to grow faster than their churches.

A leader in one of America's best-known and most highly respected interdenominational Christian organizations inflames his followers with so much hate of another Christian group that someone destabilizes. A brick finds its way through the window where the "enemy" church meets. When the believers inside the building come out to see what is going on they discover that not only were they the recipients of a brick, but the tires on all their cars have been slashed.

(Remember, all this is done to defend God.)

The leaders of a denomination, the soul of orthodoxy, launch a hate campaign against one lone church. The fires of rage are fanned so hard, so long, that the atmosphere of unmitigated hate destabilizes one member. He makes three attempts to kill the leader of the "enemy" church.

All of the above happened, happened recently, and all are right out of the middle of "mainstream" churches.

Here is a list of the general categories of the different types of churches found in North America. Let's start at the top and work down, and see which ones are and are not dangerous to be a part of.

First, there are the churches with ancient beginnings (Catholic, Episcopal). Then there are the reform churches—churches which began in Europe about four hundred years ago and were once state supported financially (Lutheran, Presbyterian).

A little lower on the pecking order you come to the more American vintage of churches: dissenters—Baptist, Congregationalist and similar type denominations. Then there are the independent congregational type churches (the Berean Bible Chapel or the New Testament Independent Bible Church just down the street from your house). Next, there is the more recent historic phenomenon of the Pentecostal-charismatic churches, some denominational, some independent and non-denominational. Down toward the bottom of the list are the non-church organizations which are often called para-church organizations. Almost at the end of the list are folks who are outside of classification. Most of these are independent churches and some are movements, but they are usually characterized by the fact that they are less than twenty years old. Other than the fact that they are new and zealous, they utterly defy classification. Some of these groups have an elitist mentality or some special doctrine or practice which characterizes them. The poor folks who belong to these colorful little movements catch more criticism and are the object of more scare tactics and witch hunts than all the rest combined. Most are utterly innocent of the stories told on them. (A few are as guilty as bandits.)

Ah, but there is yet one last kind of church on this list. You've never even heard of these people. These folks are the utterly unknown believers. (How lucky can you get!) These are believers who almost always meet in a home, and they are a part of no movement—that is, they belong to no network of churches. Most do not even have something they could call a sister church. Their organizational structure is virtually nonexistent. Some such "home churches" are very close to tribal in government, moving wholly by consensus. Such a church is truly an organic expression of the ecclesia. There is a good chance that a hundred years from now when historians are digging around in the footnotes of church history, they will declare these people to be those who, in their own century, "most reflected the spirit of the first century church."

Now, back to our question.

Which of those denominations, churches, para-churches, non-churches, etc. on our list is the most dangerous to be a member of—that is, most likely to engender a situation that produces a destabilizing atmosphere? Which group is safest? In which of them are you least likely to get hurt? Which is more likely to give you the Lord in an unadulterated way? I don't know, but judging by my mail, none of them is a sure bet.

Perhaps the worst situation I have ever come across is one that grew out of an episcopal culture, no less! Just this week a brother sent me a copy of his excommunication papers! According to his story, he had mildly disagreed with his pastor over a doctrine. He was ordered to change his view or else. He couldn't. The church council met and not only excommunicated him but declared, "We sentence you henceforth to everlasting damnation in the eternal lake of fire." And that, dear reader, was done by a mainline Presbyterian church!

All sections of the charismatic movement have more than their allotment of nightmare stories, as do the para-church organizations and the fringe movements. If my mail is any indicator, all categories of churches are potentially dangerous to your health.

What is my point? The kind of church you are in has nothing to do with how violent a church fight can get nor how dangerous one can become. Consequently, the best thing you can do for sanity and safety is not to attack anyone and not to attack another church. And if you are part of a faction within your church that is engendering hate or criticism, or is even becoming very defensive, get out fast. Get out no matter how high-soundingly orthodox the rhetoric may be, how justifiable their defense, or how worthy of everlasting perdition might appear the ones they are attacking.

Quietly remove yourself from any atmosphere of prolonged negativity and vilification. Why? Because someone could easily end up being hurt, or killed, that's why.

At the age of nineteen I stood in a pasture near the city of Zurich, Switzerland. Beside me was my seminary history professor, Dr. John Allen Moore. As our class stood in that open field Dr. Moore pointed out to us the spot where Zwingli was slain in a fierce battle fought between a Protestant army and a Catholic army. Dr. Moore explained to us that after the battle, the victorious Catholics chopped up two pigs *and* Zwingli, mingled the three together and burned them.

Now that is hate.

And it was done in the name of Jesus Christ.

(I'm not picking on the Catholics; who knows what the Protestant army might have done if it had won the battle!)

That scene, dear reader, is a pretty good picture of where just about any church split can ultimately lead.

Please reflect on this chapter. Consider the vast implications of what you are doing if you become a participant in divisiveness. Are you certain you want to be part of a church fight? Do you even want to be around when one starts?

I hope this chapter scares you. It surely scares me!

CHAPTER 5

THE NECESSITY OF TURNING CHRISTIAN AGAINST CHRISTIAN

When a split is over, why does it always end up that the ordinary Christian in the one group has no future friendships with the ordinary Christians in the other group? That may seem like an unimportant question, but the major source of energy for churches, all across the pages of history, comes out of the answer to that question. The next two chapters will give you an idea of what is really going on behind the scenes in almost every church split. And when you have finished these two chapters (which are two sides of one coin), I trust you will never want to be within driving distance of a split!

Pick up a book on church history, flip through the pages until you come to a section telling about one of those big, Christendom-wide splits. Your history book will inevitably tell you the cause of the split was "doctrinal differences." Do not be too sure. History speaks of doctrine, heresy, false teachings, differences in scriptural interpretations, and all sorts of such things as the cause of division. But are these doctrines really the cause of splits? Or is it possible they are the children of splits?

Splits father doctrines. Doctrines do not father splits. Doctrinal differences arise after the split, and they arise primarily to make sure Christians who are friends, but who happen to be in opposing camps, don't stay friends any longer!

Imagine two outstanding men. Christians. They have a disagreement. A power struggle develops. One of these men literally begins to invent teachings which are opposite to the other man's teachings. He now uses these doctrinal differences to drive a wedge between the people who are following him and the people following the other man.

You really cannot cause a split until you can first drive a wedge between *your* people and his people. Two strong men can't really split. A split comes only after a man succeeds in convincing others to follow him. Fail at gathering followers and you fail at the formation of a new work. Fail to drive a wedge between Christians and you fail at a successful split. You must attack the other man's teachings to accomplish *the ending of friendships between believers.*

To end friendships, dear reader, is the central purpose of a split. Splits only *seem* to be over doctrine. But those doctrines are there for one major reason: to divide friends. You must divide friends or your split will fail; it is that simple.

Put it another way: You are being used if you are participating in a split.

Ending friendship between people who happen to belong to two opposing groups is the key to a successful split. Doctrines are only a tool.

And now, dear reader, I would like to introduce to you some

methods you can use to end friendship and to prevent a spirit of oneness in the body of Christ. The first way? Why, with a flour sack dress, of course!

The Purpose Behind Flour Sack Dresses*

Why do you see some Christian groups wearing robes, or funny-looking or out-moded clothing? They are wearing costumes, if you please. In some of these groups the men wear beards and the women wear what look for all the world like flour sack dresses. And while we are at it, why do some Christian groups talk in a distinctive fashion? And why are some groups so exclusive, so closed off from all other Christians?

Such a group will show you a Scripture verse to justify their behavior, but the truth lies outside of Scripture. Here is the truth: The costuming of God's people reduces that people's circle of friendship fast! In fact, weird dress reduces a person's circle of friends to absolutely no one except the other people in their own little group.

Create a world in which no one has outside friends and you have eliminated almost all sources of division, temporarily at least.

Odd dress, strange costumes, a funny way to talk, an unusual vocabulary—these are a few of the ingredients of exclusivism. Is this really faithfulness to Scripture? Is this loyalty to God? It is more probable that the leader of the movement was once forced to find ways to end outside friendships so as to prevent numerical loss to another group. Ending friendships between individuals in different groups is a high priority on the list of ways to preserve unity.

(Better we have splits!)

---

*During the Great Depression, flour was sold in cotton sacks from which you could make dresses, hence the term.

The recent authoritarian movement, in embracing hierarchical authoritarianism, had its true motives somewhere other than in scriptural obedience. The true motive for the authoritarianism teaching—"Always obey the one above you"—is that to have "underlings" submit totally to "overlings" is a sure cure for splits.

Legalism, Conformity and Peculiarities

Why are some Christian groups so incredibly legalistic? Legalistic practice and mass conformity, if traced to their roots, come from the need to end division in a movement. Legalism springs from the same source as does funny talk, odd vocabulary, strange inflections, weird grammatical syntax, and peculiar dress.

Men who are insecure in their leadership know that outside friendships are the bane of unity in a movement. Such men work to eliminate such threats. Weird practices and exclusive doctrine are nothing but unwitting efforts to prevent splits.

You think this is confined to little sects that pass out tracts on the street? Well, broaden your view. How many a Baptist can you name who is a really close friend with a devout Methodist? After all, denominations do denominate.

Why do leaders build such walls? Because unity in their church is so fragile and precarious. Every church has in it all the currents, cross-currents and forces to cause a split tomorrow. A Christian worker can feel these forces at work in his church. He daily lives in the shadow of a possible split, every day of his life. And every day this worker has to crucify the temptation to come up with ways to end this potential danger. If he does not do something, soon he will find himself in a church split. So he either picks up tools that build walls to end outside friendships, or he works toward internal conformity among the believers.

I speak now to you who, seeing the shadow of a split darkening the horizon, are tempted to reach for those tools. Be advised, it takes a herculean effort to bring hate and fear to such a fever pitch as to cause friend to turn against friend. You will have to think up some doozies of accusations, doctrines, etc., in order to accomplish this feat! When it is all over, how sleeps your conscience?

Do you really want to do this?

As I stated before, here is where "doctrinal differences" really come from and why they are so fervently held. And why they are preached with such bombast and paranoia! Men must preach these "doctrinal differences" long enough, loud enough and big enough until their people believe them—strongly enough to break off lifetime friendships.

You will succeed, sir. Eventually you will obtain the results you desire. Your people will break off their friendships with your enemy and competitor. Furthermore, when you have finished your grizzly work, your people will probably do this with a vengeance!

And you will have made them tenfold more the citizens of hate than you are!

The saddest part of this whole sad scene is that no matter what a man dreams up to keep unity in his church, over the long haul it will not work. There is no such thing as a sure cure method to prevent a congregation from splitting. Some legalist in the camp is eventually going to discover grace. Someone peeks over the wall of doctrines and finds, not monsters, but brothers. Someone decides to commit the ultimate sin (even worse than witchcraft): He actually rebels and disobeys some elder, and in so doing finds freedom in Christ. Someone escapes her flour sack dress and discovers the joy of being normal. In such discoveries a split begins.

Whether you toss out your flour sack dress, or swap your legalism for grace, or give up doctrines for Lent, or—perish the thought—decide an elder has no business telling you to wash his car at three in the morning, please, dear reader, do not be the one who causes a split. And don't participate in it.

This chapter has been pretty rough on ministers. After all, is it not the minister who usually spouts doctrines, demands exclusiveness, preaches peculiar dress, invents ways to divide friend from friend, etc.? They need to stop such things, right? Ah, but this is only one side of the coin we are looking at. Turn that coin over, as we will in the next chapter, and you will discover a whole new kind of destruction coming out of the problem of friendships, and this is usually caused by laymen! You are about to discover that you, the layman, are faced with some awesome responsibilities and decisions that will affect the very survival of your church.

Welcome to the other side of the coin.

CHAPTER 6

THE DESTRUCTIVE POWER OF FRIENDSHIPS

We have seen what Christian leaders do to build walls between groups, as well as all the things they dream up to destroy friendships between Christians in different churches. Pretty bad scene, huh? Well, now you must see what happens to your church if, after a split, you persist in keeping your close friends who belong to an opposing group.

In the last chapter the Christian worker caught it for breaking up friendships. In this chapter the non-worker is going to catch it for keeping those friendships! Such a thought may come as a surprise; after all, what earthly danger is there in an innocent friendship? Even if it is a friend who just happens to dislike your church?

Well, hold onto your seat, because if you think breaking up friendships between people in opposing camps is bad, you are about to discover that keeping those friends can end up causing problems which are downright ghastly.

(I trust that by now you have noticed there is nothing decent that comes out of a church split.)

Let us say that the church you are a member of just recently went through a division. Before this split took place you decided to keep out of the line of fire. Good! But no matter how committed you are to not taking sides, when a good, old-fashioned, vicious, vitriolic split comes along—and passes—you are still headed for some of the worst days of your life.

The inevitable day must arrive when you have to begin attending the meetings of one of those two groups. Which? Regardless of which one you choose, you now face one of life's greatest traumas and one of the worst dilemmas you will ever know. Agony does not end with a split. Agony begins after a split is over.

Choose either side, and you end up facing the fact you are going to have to leave some very dear friends who meet with the other group.

Let us say you have finally made your choice. Now comes the hard part: How do you relate to your precious friends who are in that other group? A lifelong friend of yours, and one of the dearest people on earth, is in the other group. And remember, that other group is opposing your group!

Your first reaction is probably, "Well, I will just continue to be as close to my friend as I always was. Why should a church split affect my relationship to my friend?"

This you should know. If you do manage to keep your friends who are in the other group, there is an excellent chance you will do so at the cost of destroying the church you belong to!

As I said, you have only begun to know sorrow!

It is the Christian thing to do to continue friendships, is it not? You ought to continue being friends and you ought not to let division in the body affect your relationship to fellow believers, is this not true? Maybe. But it cannot always work that way. (In fact, it never works that way!)

You may not be sympathetic with the following statement, but try to be.

If you try to be friends with the "ordinary people" in that other group, you are going to destroy the group you are now in. In the process you may well destroy the Christian worker you are following. Repeat. You, dear reader, may spiritually destroy the Christian worker in your midst by keeping your friends who belong to the other group.

That is an incredible statement, is it not? Maybe you do not believe it?

Well, let us see what happens if you do keep your friends in the other group. Do you realize you will be unwittingly creating a door into your own church through which the church's enemies can enter at will?

Be sure, the "other group" is going to go through that door, which you opened, and quite literally destroy the church you belong to. If you do not think that is true, and if you do not believe such a thing could possibly happen, then you have never been a Christian worker. Any worker knows that, after a split, friendships between people in opposing camps constitute one of the worst problems any human can face.

A church literally cannot survive if the web of interlocking friendships between those two groups continues to exist.

Why?

If friendships between Christians on opposite sides of a church split do not end, one group will use those interlocking friendships as a bridge to reach Christians in the other group, and thereby continue to raid that church of its members—and to quite literally destroy the other church. "But my friend is so sweet and innocent. He would never rob people from any church."

True. But because he is your friend, that friendship will naturally cause him to meet a new friend of yours in your church, and the two of them will become friends; and the new person in your church will soon meet all his friends. Eventually, by means of this interlocking web of friendships, the new person will meet some people in the other group who will verbally rip the man who ministers to your church to shreds and who will also steal away your friend from your church.

So you thought splits weren't complicated? And dirty? And destructive? We are now looking straight into the true face of this nightmare called a church split.

(I repeat, the best way to avoid all this horror is never to split a church.)

Any worker who has even an ounce of integrity, compassion, and desire for peace would rather face just about any problem on earth than face the prospects of working his way through this hellish dilemma. What does a man do with interlocking friendships between two opposing groups?

Recently I was having lunch with a very dear friend of mine, a Christian worker from the west coast and one of the finest men I have ever known. I listened to this dear brother tell the story of what is happening in his church fellowship. As I listened, I remembered again why workers throughout church history have demanded that Christians "on their side" stop having anything to do with Christians "on the other side."

My friend is a godly, broken man, and a man of integrity and honesty. Some years ago his church went through a split. Through it all he refused to fight or do anything ugly. (That means he did nothing!) The split was, therefore, a one-sided fight. When the split was over he would not stoop to telling, or even asking, his people to stop being friends with his enemies.

And his people kept those friendships. They stayed friends with almost everyone in the other group. The results? You probably cannot believe, you probably could not even understand how unethical Christians can be. Here is what happened.

This dear Christian worker has now lost virtually his entire congregation, for the *fourth* time. The other side literally works the membership roll of his church. His enemies are forever making friends with the members of his church, then turning them against him, and then stealing them over to their church.

This dear brother does not lift a finger to stop all this. The other side keeps up a continuous raid. My friend is not going to stoop to engaging in the horrible business of making his people take sides or forcing Christians to break up friendships with other Christians. Wonderful. May there be more men like him. But be sure to add this, he is also being devoured alive. His godliness is paying off only in the destruction of his church.

What is my friend doing to himself and to his church as he walks this path of integrity? He is signing his own death warrant. He is also signing the death warrant of his church.

If any worker sits by and does not attack the men who have split his church, if he does not stop friendships by means of attack and defense, his church will be decimated. He must end friendships. If a Christian worker does nothing and says nothing, the destruction of his church is virtually assured.

I applaud the godly approach of my friend. I would that all workers would so walk. Such men are a rare breed. But the fact remains that these men must spend their lives building, and then rebuilding, and building again, ever losing to others. Each time a division comes, such men see their church brought to near annihilation.

An interlocking web of friendship between Christians who belong to two opposing groups simply means that the non-aggressive group is doomed. That fact could almost be stated as a law of nature!

A friend of mine tells of moving from Colorado just before the church he belonged to split into two groups. Years later he returned to Colorado for a visit. He discovered that each of the two opposing leaders had demanded of their people that friendships be broken off with all who were in the other faction. My friend tried to renew old friendships with people he knew in both groups. He would knock on the door of a former friend, only to be confronted. No one on either side would have anything to do with him until he declared which side he was on. Wherever he went he found bitterness and hatred. In the worst situation of all were his friends who were now in neither group; they had left both. They were too bitter and too hurt to even want to talk with him. Most of the people originally involved in the split were not following the Lord at all.

I ask you, I ask heaven, I ask earth, is division worth this price? Is preserving a group worth turning Christians into vicious, hostile adversaries?

We should not act this way. We should not force God's people into such a choice or into such a state of mind. But you, dear "lay" Christian, do have a responsibility in all this.

I have never found a Christian solution to this dilemma. Neither has my friend who has had four whole congregations robbed out from under him. Neither has anyone else. Not a Christian solution. Nonetheless, if friendships do continue between opposing groups, one group might as well close up shop. In a word, a church is virtually doomed if individual "lay" Christians keep friendships with the opposing group.

Do you wish to destroy your church just to maintain a friendship? The worker who leads your church is going to be spending the rest of his life gathering sheep for the other group if you do. Is this what you want? Don't you think that the keeping of your friends in the other group is being just a little unfair to the one who ministers to you? Your innocent friendship is destroying a Christian worker and church!

Many Christian workers have tried to operate under the impossible conditions which you and your friendships created. But the pressures of living this way are simply beyond the ability of the human fabric to endure for very long. For a man to live under such conditions, and try to preach and try to grow a church, and do so without deep physical or psychological damage, is impossible. Yet God's people blithely go on keeping friendships, watch sheep being stolen, and yet manage to believe that all this is just fine, and that the one who ministers to them should endure this crucible without even getting emotional about it!

What Christian worker who has been ministering for twenty years has not witnessed new Christians come into his church only to end up in the "other" group because of interlocking friendships? What minister, especially those in informal-type churches, has not seen a new arrival end up, often in less than a week, joining the "other group"? Life can scarcely hold a more devastating and draining experience than to see this continue day after day, year after year.

If you were a minister, and this were happening to you and to the newcomers joining your church, what would you do? Please consider that question. Please answer that question. What would you do? Here is exactly what you would do. You would fight, and the hate of hell would reign. Or you would do nothing and get so discouraged you would come down with the blind staggers.

What will most ministers do to stop this membership loss? They will declare all-out war on the other group. And God's people on both sides will be spiritually slaughtered in the process.

And if the opposite choice is made, and the minister and his church are "Christian"? The answer is simple. That is the group that is doomed. A minister faces but two possibilities: Force people to stop having anything to do with those other believers, or face certain destruction. There really are no other choices.

Well, we have now taken a good look at the problem. What of a solution?

Dear "lay" Christian, the answer is in your hands. Just what will be your attitude to brothers and sisters who leave your group? What should your attitude be toward their leader? What should be your attitude toward the Christian worker who leads your church? And what are you going to do about all those precious friends who are so dear to you, who mean you no harm, who mean your leaders no harm, but who just happen to be in that other group?

You had better come up with a good answer because you *will* face this problem. Someday. Somewhere!

Here are your choices. Harden your heart, break off the relationship you have with Christians friends in the other group, and end up being a cold, doctrine-oriented believer, shorn of all innocence...and probably wary, suspicious, and fearful.

Your other choice? Keep those friendships and watch your church be devoured because of it! And watch that situation, which you created, slowly kill your minister.

Dear reader, we have ourselves one doozy of a problem. Could Solomon tell us how to conduct ourselves in the aftermath of a split?

What would *I* do if this happened in my fellowship?

I have thought long and hard on that question. I think I would ask each Christian who wanted to keep his friends in the other group to make sure he was clear that he had made that decision on his own. After that decision was made I would back that decision one hundred percent, but I would probably also ask him to please join the other group. That is the closest I have ever come to a solution to this problem.

38

If you are going to keep your friends in the other group—the group that hates your minister—then go join the other group.

I once shared this thought with a dear Christian facing this very problem. The reaction? "I could never break up with my friends in the other group, and I could never leave my church." (So much for my solution to this problem!)

Dear reader, you have a responsibility to do one of the two. You can't keep your cake in the cake box forever and eat a piece of it every day, too. You have a responsibility. Make up your mind! Keep your friends by going with them. Or stay in your church and end this interlocking web of friendships through which the leaders of the other group will come to raid your church!

Every worker, in the aftermath of a split, must ask himself, "Do I teach my people to hate in order that we might preserve the group? Do I shear them of innocence and turn Christian against Christian in order to preserve the work?"

And every "lay" Christian, in the aftermath of a split, must ask, "Is my friendship with a Christian in the other group so important to me that I mean to keep that friendship even though it is going to make life a hell on earth for my minister, and become an instrument of destroying the church I belong to?"

Christian, make up your mind!

CHAPTER 7

THROWING OUT THE PASTOR

I will address the first part of this chapter to the pastor. But I would ask you, the laymen, to read all of this chapter, because the last half is for you.

* * *

So, dear pastor, your church is about to throw you out? It has a reputation for doing such things? Well, join the pastoral majority! Most ministers have been pressured out of a church— or thrown out—at least once in their ministry. And breathes there a church anywhere which has not turned the pressure on at least *two* of its former pastors?

First of all, do not feel too sorry for yourself; you chose to be a pastor, and this is the occupational hazard that goes with the job.

Frankly, I think the whole pastoral concept is due for a major overhaul. Just this morning I had lunch with a young man who is a new Christian, and we happened to talk about what it is like to be a pastor. This is the answer I gave to that young man.

"You are a landscape artist by trade. Try to imagine that your job is viewed in a totally different way from any other job in the world. First of all, you must always be dressed in a coat and tie during working hours. In fact you would be safer to wear it all the time, except when you shower.

"Next, remember, when you roll out of bed every day, that at each moment, today, tomorrow, and for the rest of your life, everyone who so much as sees you will be scrutinizing your every word and movement.

"Your wife must always be well groomed. And regardless of what you are (or are not) paid to be a landscaper, it is expected that your wife will always work with you, free! Everything your wife says or does will be held up to scrutiny—and probably criticized. So also your children.

"Some people are so awed by you, the landscape artist, that they back away from you when you walk into a room. Others speak to you almost in reverence. A 'normal' conversation is virtually out of the question—for the rest of your life.

"You, the local landscaper, are often lavished with praise, always received with great honor, and always treated as 'special.' You are often taken out to dinner and entertained sumptuously. You are sometimes the recipient of gifts, which, as you grow older, you come to discover are given so the persons doing the giving can later impose on your time at their choosing. (Or do they give you a gift out of some perverted, unconscious idea that if they treat you nice, they are buying God's favor?)

"But most of all, remember that it is the entire community which *pays your salary!* True, they heap praise on your work (far more than other laboring people receive). But you are also totally at their beck and call—and mercy.

"And herein lies the most unusual aspect of your vocation as a landscaper. The people in your town will probably only allow you to do business in the community for about eighteen months to three years. After that they are going to run you off.

"You see, although you are lavished with praise for your landscaping and held in highest regard as a member of the community, if you ever displease so much as even two or three people in the town, or say something they do not like, or landscape a yard in a way not quite suiting their taste, you will almost certainly lose your job. You will either be pressured out, voted out, or quietly asked to resign. (If you are a Methodist landscaper your bishop will transfer you.)

"By the way, if you are pressured out, you may be lucky to receive this week's salary check before departing. A month or two months' severance pay is out of the question. You are out on your ear, out of a job, and unwanted. You see, once you displease a people, you, dear fellow, are *persona non grata.* *

"You were received at your new job as a king. You are thrown out as a devil. If you are lucky you will find another town needing a new landscape artist. (They just threw the last one out.) When you arrive at this new town you will once more be received as a king, with both your feet firmly planted on a banana peel."

Pastor, you know all of the above is true. Not only for you, but for about three hundred thousand other Protestant ministers in this country.

There will come a time in your ministry when you tire of being treated this way. One day you become pastor of a very neat church. After a year or two there arises a small faction in the church which does not like you. They begin a campaign to pressure you out. Their reasons are ridiculous. (Chances are fair that these are some of the same people who threw out a

---

* Your presence is no longer acceptable.

43

previous pastor.) Their methods are unscrupulous. The tales told on you are utter science fiction. You are receiving some of the most unjust treatment any human ever received. You are seriously thinking about breaking this vicious cycle which pastors always find themselves in, and you are about to go on the warpath. You just may dig in your heels this time and start fighting back at the people who have started this murmuring campaign. In other words, you just may split this church right down the middle.

Hardly anyone can blame you. You do realize, do you not, that you are about to cause a church split? Do you also realize that lives are going to suffer unutterable pain and devastation? Is this really what you want to do?

Let me tell you why you *must* hand in your resignation.

You chose this life. You know that this is the way the pastoral role is played. What you are, what you do, is the modern-day practice of the pastoral concept. Until now you have played all the other parts which this role called for. You preached, visited the sick, married the young, counseled the hurting, and a thousand other things expected of the modern pastor.

The fact that there is not so much as one passage of Scripture in all the New Testament to justify the modern-day pastoral practice has nothing to do with any of this. Here is the way the present-day world sees the church leader, who happens to be called by the name "pastor." Yes, the modern-day pastoral concept began only four hundred years ago because of an odd incident which took place in Wittenburg, Germany during the Reformation, and it is not a New Testament concept. But you are still stuck with it!

You have two choices: Play the role and resign when your number is up, or go to another city, start over, taking no one with you. Those are the only two choices you have, as far as I know, that have integrity as their content. I recommend the latter. (I would suggest that when you get to that next city you start a revolution to radically alter the whole concept of the pastoral role.)

Probably you aren't too happy with either choice.

Well, look at it this way. You are the fellow up there in the pulpit telling everyone how important it is to obey the Bible, how central the Bible is, and how important it is to be a scriptural, Biblical, New Testament church. But friend, in so doing, you dig your own grave.

You bury the dead, right? Where is that in the New Testament? You marry the young, right? Where is that in the New Testament? You visit and talk sweet to little old ladies. Where is that...oh well, you get my drift. The coat and tie. A set salary every week, with someone else in control of when (and if) you get that salary. The church building. Even the pulpit, choir and—heaven forbid—even the Sunday morning worship service. And the Sunday sermon and the rhetorical art and style by which you deliver that sermon. All these concepts came out of the Reformation, not the New Testament. The church building, of course, was invented single-handedly by Constantine in exactly 323 A.D. In fact, the whole concept of "pastor" hangs on one little word in a long string of words found in Ephesians, combined with an accident of history in around 1530.

Dear fellow minister of the Gospel, you have a totally untenable, wholly unworkable, scripturally indefensible job!

Consider this.

You have been hired to proclaim boldly the Gospel, fearlessly, dauntlessly, uncompromisingly, to a people who are staring at you while sitting immobile on hard wood. Of course they hired you to preach, and to do so fearlessly, uncompromisingly, etc. But at the same time there is an unwritten law that you are never to say anything that offends their very sensitive sensibilities. And if you do happen to do such a dastardly

45

thing, they are going to take your salary away from you. That is a very unworkable relationship. But you agreed to it!

Take another look at the pastoral role as it is presently practiced. It has not a single verse in the New Testament willing to justify its existence. Step back and look at the origins of most of what you do, then take another look at the fine print in the job description. The whole concept is unworkable and quite close to a study in madness! There is nothing in Christendom that needs so radical a reworking as the modern day practice of pastor. Nonetheless, it is the job description of a position you accepted. Now friend, it is time to go. So tell your wife to get out the suitcases and start packing.

(Are you sure you don't want to go start a revolution instead?)

A parting word of advice. Every preacher on earth ought to be required to have a job skill. There are two reasons. First, when they throw you out, you can ease the trauma and provide for your family's support by being able to go out and get a job. Secondly, if you know you can walk away from the pulpit you now occupy and make a living the next day, man, will you ever preach more boldly than you would under any other conditions!

Lastly, if you ever do have the privilege of starting a church, do not get yourself in the position that Baptist preachers are in because we believe in a congregational church government. Never get yourself in a position where you are salaried. What should you do instead? *Don't ask me, I work for a living.* But surely there must be a better way than having an income that is subject to the whims of a few super-sensitive folks.

* * *

Now to the laymen involved in pressuring the pastor out of a church.

There is really no way to describe how untenable your position is from the viewpoint of Scripture. No, we do not find the concept of the present-day pastoral practice in Scripture. But when you come to the idea of deacons or elders (or even Aunt Nina) forcing a pastor to leave the church, even a chimpanzee could tell you there is no such practice in the New Testament. You have not a scriptural leg to stand on.

Actually churches don't throw out pastors; strong-willed men and women do. Businessmen especially have a bad habit of leading a pastoral ouster. Some seem to think that being financially successful in business somehow proves them to be smarter than other folks. (Actually, it is a matter of different values, not always of intelligence. You succeed in business because that is what is important to you. Others of us deliberately choose to invest our time elsewhere.)

A few days ago I was talking to one of the district superintendents of the Methodist Church. It is the district superintendent who moves pastors from one church to another. I posed this question to him: "In your district, have you noticed it is usually the same churches who, over and over again, become dissatisfied with their pastor and request a new one?" His answer was an obvious "yes." But the thought came to me that such a church did not see itself that way at all. It was, after all, the *pastor's* fault that the pastor got pressured out.

Sir, there is simply no way to explain to you how unethical, fleshly, reprehensible, unchristian and downright loathsome is your conduct when you start murmuring in your church or become part of a discontented faction.

And look at your reason for getting rid of a pastor. Here are the typical ones. (None this side of adultery is really acceptable.) He's boring, ill-mannered, too fat, too skinny, too loud, too quiet, too bold, too meek, too young, too old. But worse than all these sins, he hurt Aunt Nina's feelings.

A wise man was once asked in my hearing, "Why do churches fight?" His answer was as quick as lightning. "Because of our love for the Lord!" After a moment of stunned silence he was asked to explain his incomprehensible answer. Here was his answer.

"Oh yes. I love the Lord too much for you to do this to our church. I love the Lord too much for you to teach this to God's people. I love the Lord too much to see you change a church my father helped build. I love the Lord too much for you to tear out those stained glass windows with my great grandparents' names on them."

When you throw out a pastor, you love the Lord and your church too much.

What you should do, but probably will not do, is to quietly leave, taking no one with you. But no doubt you will find throwing him out to be less inconvenient than leaving the church you revere so much. Never mind that your actions will be ugly, vicious, and unchristian. Never mind that you will destroy people's spiritual lives. What matters is your feelings.

You, and thousands of men and women like you, will go on throwing pastors out until the day the modern practice of the ministry is utterly ended. But what bothers many of us is not primarily the fact that the pastor is thrown out, but the unmitigated hate and the desire to inflict the absolute maximum pain and vengeance.

To what do I refer? Many things, but the one that comes to mind first is how a church lets its pastor leave town. Virtually any pastor who has been forced out of a church can tell you he resigned on Sunday, picked up his check for that week's salary, and by Monday's dawn he was on his own. Any church that squeezes a pastor out, leaving him no place to go, ought to give him a minimum of two months' severance pay...regardless of the circumstances surrounding his leaving.

I leave you with a question. Does your concept of Jesus Christ allow you to run off a pastor? Is that your understanding of the ethics of Jesus Christ?

In the meantime, let us all look forward to the day when the present-day concept of the pastoral ministry vanishes off the face of the earth!

CHAPTER 8

DO IT MY WAY

Splits come in all shapes and sizes, so to try to picture a "typical" division is impossible. But I would like to talk about one of the major root causes behind many splits.

Churches have problems because of people's dispositional differences. By dispositional difference I mean their likes, their dislikes, their inclinations. Out here where I live, in the unstructured world of "church life," most of those who come together with other believers are sincerely seeking after a true, practical expression of the body of Christ. Nonetheless each person "sees" the body of Christ, the church, through his own unique disposition.

Every Christian worker will immediately recognize what I am referring to. As a Christian worker deals with a myriad different people, he begins to see that each has a slightly different pattern of living, thinking, and seeing.

(Woe to that poor, ignorant minister who tries to conform all these people out there in his congregation to *his* disposition!)

Right over there sits a Christian who wants a church that emphasizes *evangelism.* But over here is a Christian who wants the church to place great emphasis on *prayer.* That fellow back there wants the church to address *current issues* (abortion, minority discrimination, etc.). See that Christian sitting about midway? Well, he wants *home life,* family life, and child-rearing to be the central focus of the church. The fellow on the second row? He wants everyone to have a closer involvement in one another's lives, to build *relationships.*

The list of the different interests which come out in a congregation is long, perhaps even endless. I would like to list a few just so you can see what we are up against.

Not one item on this list is really there because it is "what the Bible teaches." It is, rather, an "I want the church to be like this" list. And the list grows longer every time someone new joins the fellowship!

These are the last days. Emphasize the Lord's return.

We need miracles, healings, power, signs, wonders.

Let's get into the casting out of evil spirits and warfare with the enemy.

Let's have a loving church, everyone caring for one another, everyone getting to know one another closely.

We must confess needs to one another.

Here are some more:

Authority and submission

Shepherding and elders

Freedom, no authority. And no elders

Counseling

Missions

Doing good, helping the needy in the community

The deeper life

Visiting the sick, caring for the aged, taking care of parents, visiting those in jail

Going to meetings

Not going to meetings

More ministry

Less ministry

Singing

Less singing

Living in common

Not living in common

Sin

Confession

Prophesying over one another and telling one another, "The Lord spoke to me about you." (You have a secret sin in your life and the Lord has told me that your punishment is that you are about to be hit by a meteor from Jupiter!)

Purity, holiness

Young people

Children

Singles

Marrieds; husband-wife relationship

Money, learning a skill or vocation, the Christian in the work place

Liberal causes

Conservative causes

Training young workers in the church

No training of young workers in the church, "go somewhere else besides the church to train workers"

Tongues and interpretation

Rebuking, exhorting, confronting

Being sweeter, nicer, more loving toward one another. Less confrontation

Bible study

Even **more** Bible study

A **Christian** school - Christian education (let's start with elementary school, then a junior high, then a high school)

No! No Christian school sponsored by the church.

Getting all believers together, oneness of the body. (Let's go talk to all the pastors in town about dropping their denominating.)

Revival

Attack the religious system

Love the religious system

The world is going to pot, we should all move to northern Alaska or the South Pole.

Each one of these people sees the thing he is asking for as absolutely central. Or awfully close to it! Each sees his interest as one of the great themes of the Bible. One way or the other about half the people in the church want more (or less) emphasis on something!

No wonder we have splits!

There are the needs, the likes, the dislikes, the preferences of: the marrieds, the singles, the brothers, the sisters, the strict, the loose, the mindy, the emotional, the doer, the feeler, the objective, the subjective, the "let's move," the "let's stay put," the leader, the rebel, the follower, the critical, the professionally disgruntled, the old, the young, the children, the fellow forever asking questions, the sweet, the bold, the scared, the fearless, those needing more home life, those with financial needs, the rich, the poor. Those with a burning vision. Those who just cannot see such a vision. And on it goes.

And in the midst of all these demands, requests and counter-requests stands one befuddled, bemused and sometimes quite awed Christian worker, trying to figure out how to say grace over all this.

It is a wonder the church of God doesn't split more!

Take note, dear reader (for you may not be aware), every day a Christian worker feels the presence of these different currents pressing in on him, pulling him one way, then the other. This sense of conflicting forces stays with a minister almost every moment of his life. Somehow, the man tries (valiantly, and usually in vain) to see that everyone's needs are addressed. He misses a few. Some needs get totally overlooked. A few are overemphasized. Some are emphasized and then forgotten.

Generally, the Lord's people are patient. Almost everyone in the church finds himself spending most of his time waiting in line to see his need, his vision, his wants addressed. But every once in a while someone does not see his "vision" as a dispositional need which is part of his personality. He sees his need as a need of all Christendom. Right now!

> "It should be our number one task. And furthermore, sir, this is what everyone in the church wants. We are all talking about it. All of us. And we want it now."

Maybe he doesn't quite say it that emphatically, but look in his eyes, watch his body language, the tone of his voice. That is what he is saying. With or without words.

And, dear Christian worker, when you hear the tomtom beating out this message, you are in trouble.

Perhaps it is only an individual who has said this. Maybe it is not too late for something to be worked out. But the possibility of a firestorm is upon you.

What shall the Christian worker do at this moment?

When a crisis begins to build, I'll tell you exactly what the worker is thinking. "Why don't you go somewhere else and build a church your way!"

Unfortunately, very few men would heed such a word. Most men would even be shocked at the thought. Most Christians know they cannot leave this church and go out and, single-handedly, build a church from scratch. They probably never once thought in those terms. They just want to tell *their Christian worker* how to do it, according to *their* architectural plans.

Most Christians would be horrified at the idea of walking into another town and starting a meeting of Christians, raising up the church and molding it into the near-perfect reality of their own vision.

Could *you* pull off such a thing, dear reader?

Can you—right now—move to another town, alone, and raise up a church, lead it to experience some rich, new, higher church life? Can you, singlehandedly, bring your vision of what a church should be into reality?

If so, go. (And take no one with you!)

Oh, but you like it here? And there isn't a church anywhere living out your vision? And you can't see yourself starting one? Then have you ever thought about being just a little more quiet?

Dare you press a Christian worker to use his gift (given to him from God) to do your bidding? Is the gift of God supposed to be rented out? A minister of the Gospel cannot turn over the gift and calling of God, nor the fire which burns in his bones, to build a church according to your liking. The worker is being asked (or told?) to use his gift and call, his God given ability, to build according to someone else's vision. And to act in such a way that his personality does not offend others. Frankly, a lot of church complaining boils down to, "Preacher, I don't like your personality. Change it to suit me, or get out." Well, the fact is that nobody on earth can change his personality to suit your taste, especially a minister of the Gospel!

But more important—and please, dear reader, hear this—a Christian worker cannot use his call, his gift, his heart...to accomplish *your* dream. A worker cannot do that which is not his passion. Why, then, hold him responsible for not doing the thing you see needs to be done? Especially if you know good and well you yourself could not go start a church and accomplish this vision of yours.

Please use this as your measuring stick: Can I leave this church, taking no followers, go to another city, and raise up a church and lead an entire congregation in all it should be?

If the answer is no, then relent in pursuing your view. If you cannot relent, and the problem is eating a hole in you, then you might wish to consider leaving. (Quietly!)

You have three choices. 1) Split the church. 2) Go somewhere else, alone, and build a church that is after your desire. 3) You might choose to take yourself and your frustrations to the cross and there let them be crucified. If you cannot handle any of the above, the most beneficial thing you can do for all concerned is quietly leave.

Whatever you choose, don't dismember the body of Christ over your desire to have things your way.

CHAPTER 9

STYLE

Perhaps the last chapter did not strike you as practical. You wish to stay in your present church and to have your view attended to. Then consider two things. One is *style*, the other is your *track record*. The way you approach other people about your view is important. Style becomes very important. (This is true even in the way you approach a preacher!) If you are rude, insulting, pushy, absolute, or insistent, you may run into a bit of a problem trying to get the worker (or anyone in the church) to go down the road of your desires.

Christian workers are human. Very human. Like anyone else a worker can get his feelings ruffled. As Shakespeare expressed (*The Merchant of Venice*), "If you hit us will we not feel pain? If you cut us will we not bleed? If you poison us will we not die?" A minister of the Gospel can be hurt, feel pressure, feel put upon, and—believe it or not—can sometimes feel a little insecure. Especially in the presence of an aggressive or demanding approach, or any approach that seems threatening to him.

"Be sweet to me and I'll be sweet, too" was a comment I once heard from a wise man seeking to make this very point. The words sound juvenile, but they are still true. Come in with threatening, demands, pressures, or even an unhappy look, and your chance of getting your way drops to nil...with anyone, not just a worker. Style is important.

The other factor that may be considered important is your past track record. If your past record indicates you are aggressive, an old grump, a chronic complainer, a demander, a fault-finder, a dominator, a gossip, or one forever sprouting ideas which others ought to carry out; if you get fired easily, or are hard to work with, then two things are clear: First, your chances of being heard are less than nil. (Sorry, that is just the way the rest of the human race naturally reacts to your sort.) Secondly, any worker who has been in the Lord's work for over fifteen minutes will, consciously or unconsciously, look upon you as a potential church splitter!

If your style is one that is positive and bespeaks of up-building the body, you should get a pretty good reception in most church fellowships. If you do not? Then the place is probably not worth your efforts anyway. And it sure ain't worth splitting.

If your style is less than positive, and if your wheel is invariably squeaking, you are apt to note that some quiet little brother or sister (who comes up with about one suggestion per year) gets his way in the blink of an eye and all you get is the thousand-yard stare.

If it happens that both your style and your track record are poor, you are probably going to feel very alone most of your life.

I have a list of things which I would like to see become reality in the church. I also have a list of things I hope never to see introduced into the church. There are other Christian workers who could read my list and agree with none of it. (And they each have a couple of lists too!) Then there is your list. The question is not my list, his list or your list. The question is, will you split a church because the worker in your midst will not respond to your list?

One other word. Be wise. Never say to a worker, "A lot of other people feel the same way I do." You may believe this will cause him to think, "Wow, it's a wave, I'd better do it!" Rather, he will be thinking, "Good grief, he's going door to door promoting his ideas!"

The problems and the needs which a church has do not split churches. The believer who demands his way is what splits churches. Be content to see just a little bit accomplished in the areas of your burning heart. A tiny bit! At best, none of us see even a fraction of what we hope for actually come to pass in the life of the church.

Remember, for every one hundred people in your church there are also one hundred different dispositions, one hundred different sets of likes and dislikes. None of us will ever get much of our way.

And when someone does start pushing hard for his way and begins to promote discord, I trust that you, dear reader, will pass up the opportunity to let his dispositional tendencies cause a church schism.

CHAPTER 10

RAIDS

"Church split" has a cousin named "church raid." A raid is almost, but not quite, the same as a split. A split is a conflagration which involves a whole church. A raid is smaller. And a raid can be so quick and quiet that many in the church never even know one has taken place. It can actually begin and end in one weekend!

But a raid can also move agonizingly slowly, starting imperceptibly, appearing ever so spiritual, then going on interminably before it can finally be labeled a certified *raid.*

A raid can usually be described as one man leading off a handful of people. Whatever its style, a raid still amounts to robbery.

Perhaps the greatest damage done by raids is they can discourage a church so much that, if enough of them happen, they take the very heart out of a church.

Who does the raiding?

The best answer is, raids are led by Christians who are looking for a group of people they can lead. Secondly, the person leading the raid and looking for a following vows (1) he is not leading a raid and (2) he is not looking for a following. That is a classical raid. (Those following him vow they are not following him and are not being raided!)

What we have, then, is a non-leader who takes away non-followers which causes a non-split. That is a raid.

An interesting curiosity about many raids is that the leader of the raid so often uses the following statement to lead people out: "We Christians should not have leaders. Only the Lord should lead us." For some reason this idea really is appealing. The tragedy is, of course, they follow the man who teaches it.

If I had a dollar for every man who raided a church by saying, "We are not going to have a leader, we are only going to follow Christ," I could probably come close to single-handedly paying off the national debt. (Well, at least the interest payment.) This is the most frequently used ploy of men looking for followers. Not only is it not honest, not scriptural and not workable, but it is virtually always a lie of the heart. I would implore you, dear reader, never to listen to a man who plays this flute. Those who follow this tune end up in a disaster.

One thing is certain. Poll all those who are listening, and they will tell you that this brother who is raising these issues is doing so out of a pure heart.

These dear, innocent believers do not realize they are caught up in a drama as old as Christianity, a drama which will be relived in ten thousand Christian gatherings this year!

One other thing they don't realize. They have no idea how deeply this coming division is going to hurt, nor how many it will hurt. I have stated earlier that a *Christian* can usually survive only two or three splits in one lifetime. In the same way a *church* can go through just so many raids before that church reaches a point of discouragement from which it is almost impossible to recover.

A rotten soul dwells within that man who brings division to someone else's gathering! He is not worthy to be followed. Most such men will say, "I only wanted to help, to change; I had no desire to divide. But they wouldn't listen. Look what they did to me!" Or, they will say, "The man leading us was wrong. He should never have begun that work. It was not worthy to go on. I had to stop it." "They were teaching heresy." "They were not organized enough." "They were too organized." "The people who left would have left anyway." "We came in peace and were not heard."

It does not matter what words you hear him say; neither he nor you—nor anyone—has any business bringing division to a body of believers.

Recognize that splits and raids do happen, often! And let us all stop being part of them.

CHAPTER 11

ANATOMY OF A RAID

You are about to read two stories, both about a raid on a church. The first is told to illustrate what a raid is like. The second is told in order to...well, we will come to that a little later. (Expect a surprise ending!)

* * *

He called long distance almost every day. Age twenty-two. Eager. Excited. He wanted to move across America to be in that wonderful church, and to come live in a house filled with single brothers. It seemed to those who spoke with him by phone that a very special young man was about to arrive; after all, he called so often, asked so many questions, seemed so interested. No one noticed that all his questions allowed him to time his arrival to coincide with the arrival of seven other young people who were coming in from different parts of the country.

He had been there only three days when he asked all the other young men living in the "single brothers" house to meet with him so he could share with them a burden he had. He sensed some problems, he said. He began by assuring everyone he was not being critical; he gave this assurance again and again. He was still giving that assurance into the wee hours of the night as he blasted the church from one end of logic to the other. He questioned whether or not this fellowship even had a right to exist, and branded the whole thing as "not of God."

He soon had everyone in the room frightened out of their wits. He undermined, if not outright destroyed, all the trust in the hearts of those young men. Before dawn had arrived almost all of them were considering leaving. Where would they go? Why, wherever *this young man* was going.

Remember, he was only twenty-two.

The next day the owner of the house, having found out what was going on, asked him to move out. His reaction:

> I was **not** being critical.
> My motives were pure.
> I meant no harm.
> I am being persecuted—unfairly.
> Your asking me to leave is proof of all I accused you
> of.

The reaction of the other young men?

> He is pure in his motive.
> He was not being critical.
> He did not influence any of us; we were already
> having our own doubts.
> You are asking him to move out? That is unchristian
> and outrageous. Besides, he is doing no harm.

Even as he packed to move he kept up his barrage of accusations. Nor did he actually leave. He checked into a nearby motel and continued talking by telephone to the young men living in the house.

In all this the young man maintained his purity of motives and innocence of heart. When finally he was gone, he had taken one person with him and left five others utterly confused. The heart had gone out of the house. Soon those five left too.

But that is not all. An entire church went into a depression. It is only human, getting depressed in the midst of a raid. Or two raids. Or three. The depression grows more acute each time a church passes through such a scenario.

Now, here is the other story. It sounds almost exactly like the one above, except for one rather unusual difference.

This young man was also twenty-two years old. He, too, had moved halfway across America to be with a wonderful church, and to live in a house full of single brothers. After being around for about four months, he began passing out some rather unusual literature to the young men he lived with. Soon he was talking to the more impressionable young men in the fellowship about many of his beliefs.

Growing a little bolder as his influence grew, he began sharing his teaching with new people as soon as they joined this fellowship. In fact he got to know the new arrivals faster than anyone else, going to their homes, spending time with them, and, eventually, sharing his beliefs. He even began his own meeting in the home of one of the newcomers.

One night in a meeting he prayed for the fire of God to come out of heaven and burn up this church. (In all the places where he had done this before—he later declared—God had destroyed those groups. No exceptions!)

A few days later, he took four young men with him to a conference of a movement which taught his beliefs. Well, the folks in the church were growing a little impatient, disturbed, sad and discouraged by all these things. He was asked to take thirty days to decide if he wished to continue living with the young men he lived with, and then to decide if he really belonged in this fellowship. Can you guess his reactions?

He protested his innocence.

He vowed purity of heart.

He declared he was being persecuted.

He immediately left and took five young people out with him! As they departed all six protested his innocence, his purity. All agreed he was being persecuted. All stated they were not being influenced by him. (Haven't we heard this somewhere before?)

By the way, an interesting question was put to him, since so many were non-following him. The question was, "If you had never been born, would these other young men be leaving?" His reply was given with utmost confidence: "Absolutely!" He really didn't believe he had been the cause of these people's leaving!

And what is the surprise ending?

During the entire chain of events recorded above, this young man, and all the other young men who followed him, were reading a rough draft of *this book!* Now that could discourage a large granite boulder, couldn't it?

My point? *Nothing* is going to stop some people from causing splits and raids. And *never* will they admit they are causing that split.

There is no way to prevent some splits. All that can be done is for *you* to have nothing to do with one, ever!

CHAPTER 12

CHARACTERISTICS OF A RAID

In my lifetime I have traveled across a large part of this planet. Most of North America is almost as familiar to me as my back yard. In the process of these travels I have had the privilege of visiting many home groups and informal, unstructured churches. Without exception every one of those fellowships has been raided...almost annually! (The majority of them have also known at least one traumatic split.) Mind you, these are precious, innocent groups, not some large movement or denomination. These folks are the dearest and the best believers there are on this earth.

I have sat in the midst of these precious little fellowships and listened to dear Christians (and broken-hearted workers) tell their tales of being raided. Again and again.

Innocent, impressionable (and usually young) Christians being led off by one who sells dreams is a common occurrence in Christian groups, especially those groups with an atmosphere of freedom, who meet informally. Unfortunately there is a host of people (young, old and middle-aged) who see such informal churches as a happy hunting ground from which to collect followers. In these churches they attempt to pull off shenanigans they would never dream of trying in a traditional church setting.

So has it ever been, so shall it ever be.

Recalling to mind the innumerable stories these believers have shared, I have gleaned from them a few points which seem to be common to all. Here they are.

The one who is leading a raid, if he is stopped at any point before he actually overtly leaves with his stolen sheep, will always declare that he is totally innocent and falsely accused.

Secondly, just about everyone in the church will believe him; even those who do not follow him. Stop that fellow before he brings his raid to a clear-cut climax and everyone will think him both innocent and mistreated! This leaves the church's leadership with no real *Christian* alternative but to let the raid run its full course. Stop the raid at any time before he leads his followers out the door and you will look like a double-dirty villain.

I believe the term to describe the dilemma that the church's leadership faces is "hanged if you do, hanged if you don't." There is *no* solution to this dilemma. You can't handle a problem like this without profound repercussions, no matter what you do!

Thirdly, the man leading the raid often plays the role of one who is simply too spiritual to criticize his persecutors, even while criticizing them. Either way, the church's leaders, if they dare try to stop him, get hung out to dry.

Next, those following him out the door will vow they are in no way being influenced by him. Never have I heard a Christian who admitted that he was following the person leading a raid. That includes people who have moved across a continent in order to non-follow this non-guilty man who is a non-leader of a non-split.

The next one is as invariable as the rotation of the planets: After the raid the ones departing will continue their friendships with Christians in the church which they split!

This last one creates a great problem in the church that has been raided. In fact, this situation leaves a church's leadership facing one of the most difficult problems ever to face a Christian.

Oh, yes, there is one last characteristic common to all these stories I have heard. It is so important, it deserves a chapter in itself.

CHAPTER 13

ONE INGREDIENT COMMON TO ALL SPLITS

I have been studying church history since I was seventeen years old, which was a long time ago. In the process of these studies I have read numerous accounts of court trials of so-called heretics. (These are actual courtroom procedures against faithful believers who were dragged into court for being heretics, if you please!) Invariably, when standing before either a secular or a religious court of law, these dear saints were found guilty and sentenced to prison or death because the court ruled that they were *not fit to live.*

Some of these dear believers were ordered to be roasted alive, slowly. Others were to have their flesh torn from their bodies with red-hot tongs while walking to the place where they were to be burned alive. Others died by even more terrible means. All these believers, mind you, were killed by Christians...to preserve the Christian faith from being perverted.

How, you ask yourself again and again, could religious men, men who confess faith in Christ, do such things to other human beings?

The answer is simple. In every age, in every century, in every decade, in every land, you will find this one statement made by the Christians who were condemning "heretics" to annihilation:

"*God* has shown us that you are not fit to live."

In every really first class split I have heard about, there comes a moment when the leader declares that God told him that the church he is splitting was not worthy to exist. (His words may be a little different from that. He may say it is a cult. Or this church is teaching a heresy. Or this church is not of God.)

Of course with God on your side, anything is ethical, is it not?

Those leading a split have to believe that God is finished with the church they are ripping to shreds. This alone can justify the conduct they are engaging in. When God tells *you* such a thing, and you launch a split, *or join* a split, you, sir, have become part of the company of men who burn other men at the stake!

Did God speak? Or is the man leading the split simply driven by frustration, or maybe even hate?

Let's say you are the one splitting the church. Let's say you happen to have a sound mind and are psychologically balanced. Let's say God really did tell you He is finished with this church. Let's go further, let's say the whole crowd down there at that "church" really are a bunch of heretics. If that is the case, you need to ask yourself, "If they are heretics, just how good is my judgment about *anything?* After all, I joined them!" Is your judgment about their heresy better than your original judgment in deciding to join up with them? If they are heretics, does that fact justify your causing a split? Friend, if they are as black-hearted as you suppose them to be, slip out the door and never tell anyone you ever heard of them!

If you do decide to split that group, you do realize, do you not, that you may have to stand before your Lord one day. And at that moment you may find you need one long, tall explanation about the hidden motives of your heart!

Remember, this century's heretic is next century's hero!

I will repeat myself, dear reader. You ought never to follow a man who splits (or raids) a professing group of Christians, nor should you attack another group of professing believers. And beware the man who has a negative word from God about a church.

You, sir or madame, should never raid or split a group of professing believers, *no matter what the circumstances.* And your definition of heresy, and your conviction that the people you oppose are heretics, creates no exception.

We simply have no business sowing discord in any group of people.

And be done with the statement, "That group has no right to exist." Leave that statement to the savage pages of history when men lived in the Dark Ages.

CHAPTER 14

PERIPHERAL CHRISTIANS

Now I would like to introduce you to the wonderful world of Christians who live out there on the edge of church life! They are a powder keg once a split begins. You don't know what a problem is until you try to find a *Christian* way to deal with *peripheral* Christians.

If you belong to a more traditional-type church you may hardly be aware of "peripheral Christians." But in the less formal churches these people are the bane of our lives. A traditional church holds forth mainly on Sunday morning, in a highly structured meeting. The believers in informal churches, on the other hand, become very involved with one another in day-to-day fellowship. Obviously, most Christians prefer the more formal, less personal type church. Some simply want to check in on Sunday at eleven and check out at noon. Anyway, the "peripheral mentality" is almost universal in Christianity.

Almost.

The exception is those informal churches which meet in living rooms. These people are usually a very committed bunch of believers. These folks are not peripheral Christians. Unfortunately, every once in a while a peripheral Christian stumbles upon the "home church" believers. Boy, do they like what they see! (And do they mess things up!)

Peripheral Christians really love these lively, informal meetings. (Living room kind of meetings are almost always zippier than those held in the more traditional church building.) And the sharing, and the singing and the message. They are crazy about the singing, the people, the depth in the message they hear preached. "Wow," say the peripheral Christians. "I've never seen anything like this!" They will definitely be back next week!

Sadly, these folks want only to trip merrily into the meeting, grab the goodies and the glory, and trip merrily out again. No commitment. No involvement. "Meeting sippers!"

This type of mentality knows no cure.

If you happen to be such a Christian, what you want (in a nutshell) is to warm your hands and heart at the glories of LIFE, joy at unbelievable revelation, then go home and go to bed. That's it! Until next Sunday.

You, sir, are the curse of church life!

Why? Because (1) you are so determined to get all the blessings, and (2) you are just as determined to remain uncommitted. And, it turns out, your greatest single expenditure of energy is to convince us to adopt your view of commitment. Your view of commitment, by the way, is to be uncommitted. No matter what your conduct, no matter what you do or say, you want the Christian worker who is leading the group to never ask you to give up your fence-sitting habits.

You want that worker to preach the most powerful revelation in church history, and you want him back next week (and every week!) doing more of the same. You want to see him up there preaching the outer limits of revelation regardless of how much your complacency drags the church down. And the minister must never get discouraged even though he sees *you* digging a hole in which to bury the very purpose for which the church exists.

You never knew a yawn could be so powerful, did you? Let's just see what peripheral Christians do to a truly committed body of believers.

Peripheral Christians Breed!

Into a glorious home meeting steps the peripheral Christian for the first time. He is absolutely crazy about all the love and caring and fellowship he observes. You see, the peripheral Christian likes people. Fellowship seems to be his middle name. Furthermore, he loves the Lord...in his fashion. And at first glance, he looks committed.

Sure enough, "Peripheral Christian" comes back to more meetings. Soon he is warming his hands almost full time at the fire of church life. What he does not realize is that these people are pouring the whole of their lives into their church, and that is what makes the meetings so incredibly glorious. A peripheral Christian will die and go to heaven having never grasped this fact.

Glory, light, joy, fellowship—that is what he wants, and effortlessly. Spiritual expenditure is not in his computer banks.

One good thing can be said for the peripheral Christian, though; he loves to make friends. You might call this his magnificent obsession. Soon he knows everyone in the church, visits all the homes, joins in all the fellowship.

But in a meeting he either sits in the rear, listening, but saying and doing nothing, or he shares...and shares and shares. And shares...with a shallowness that reflects the lack of spiritual depth in his life. He is a parasite, drawing his life from others.

This fellow is not only not committed, he is committed to not being committed. He never really learns what the group is about—its purpose, its hope, its dream, its passion!

If it all stopped here perhaps we could figure out a way to contain this soul. Unfortunately, though, this fellow breeds his kind. He has twins, sisters, brothers, cousins—all sorts of kinfolk. Soon the meeting is full of these folks. They are multiplying like rabbits. Their creed is, "We want a place where there is a great performance, great preaching and great singing, but where commitment is not demanded."

If the other people in a highly committed church are not careful, they will wake up one day to discover their church has a ratio of five uncommitted Christians to every one committed. And growing!!

The Peripheral Christian and His Right to Criticize

You who belong to the company of the uncommitted and who forever stand on the outer edge, the longer you are around the more you consider it your right to voice opinions on what this church is, its purpose, and its level of commitment.

"I reserve the right to consider myself one of you, to be critical of anything you do, and to make friends with your enemies and introduce others in the group to your enemies. Never criticize me for doing these things."

The Peripheral Christian's Role in a Church Split

Now let us see the role of a peripheral Christian during a church split. He certainly does not start the split. That takes effort! But in the middle of a split he says, "I reserve the right to be part of a split, to join the other group when they leave, to criticize you, and to continue meeting with you! Yes, I intend to help the split, and still keep meeting with *you,* the very people I split away from."

You may not believe what you just read, but it is true. This fellow helps split the church, and still wants to keep attending the meetings! And he expects to be received and loved, with no censure of his conduct.

Now, dear reader, you have at last met the peripheral Christian. If you were a Christian worker, what would you do with folks who consider you an old ogre if you even think of stopping them from splitting the church *and* still attending it? That is, what would you do that could be classed as charitable?

The peripheral Christian is a ticking bomb in any Christian group. It seems to be his nature to go with dissenters. But here is his greatest danger. He is adamant in his demand to keep all of his friendships in the group he split.

Is your church an unusual dynamo of life? Is the number of peripheral Christians increasing? Success may be about to sink your church's standards! When you start picking up these once-a-week folks, the science of church splits says *you have just added one of the major ingredients for a split.*

There is only one way that I know to defuse the influence of peripheral Christians, and that is to start a church made up of peripheral Christians! Major in having a church that has lots of "life" to it, but really doesn't expect much from its members beyond "going to church on Sunday morning." You should be able to go at least two hundred years without a split!

Otherwise, if the number of Christians "with their hands in their pockets, leaning up against a post" is growing, a split is probably coming!

If you do have a large periphery group in your church and if—in a fit of sanity—you try to rid your church of the peripheral Christians, *for sure* a split is coming!

There is a lesson which I have learned as a teacher in public schools. Always listen to the noise level in the classroom and know that, if the noise in the room reaches a certain threshold, either a fight will break out or someone will be hurt. Or both.

A similar thing can be said in the science of church splits. If a truly living body of believers acquires a large periphery, that church will soon have a split. Don't ask me why, it is just true.

The Christian Worker and the Peripheral Christian

Does a peripheral Christian have a scriptural right to exist? What a question. I just wish I knew the answer! If he does not, what do you do with him? If he does, where is his place? Does he have a right to be in a body of committed believers? If not, how do you keep him out? And if he is already in, what civilized means do you have to get rid of him? If he does have a right to be part of a truly committed body of believers, what on earth do you do to keep him from ruining that body of believers?

Is there anybody out there who has a genuinely Christian, non-legalistic, non-sectarian, non-harsh answer to this question?

This dilemma of what to do with peripheral Christians constitutes one of the major agonies of a Christian worker. When a Christian worker is trying to raise up a pure, innocent, decent, open, non-sectarian, non-legalistic work, how does he deal with the peripheral Christian? That is, how can he deal with such people without the worker himself becoming impure, legalistic, sectarian, harsh, mean, angry, etc.? What can a minister of the Gospel do, in working with peripheral Christians, that is not legalistic, not damaging to their lives, but which will cause them to get "in" or "out"?

If you really have a practical, working, non-theoretical answer to that question, let us all know. Quick!

I trust that you are beginning to grasp the complexity and danger that comes with having uncommitted Christians in your church. In the next chapter we discover yet one more danger these folks pose. In fact, the greatest danger of all.

CHAPTER 15

CHRISTIANS WHO KILL THE PURPOSE OF THE CHRUCH

Now we come to the very center of the heartbreak caused by the peripheral Christian. If given a choice I would gladly go through a split rather than go through the greater agony of watching a church die because of the influence which peripheral Christians weave into the fabric of a church.

Point: Peripheral believers water down the very purpose for which a group of committed believers exists. The church's standard drops through the floor with an influx of the lukewarm. The more of them, the lower the standard drops.

Here is what happens if you try to cure the problem. You call the church together and explain to everyone the original purpose for which this church came into existence. You describe the standard with which it began. Then you ask those present to consider this standard and either get off the fence or "go join some nice, lukewarm, dead, Baptist church."*

(You realize, of course, this statement is a terribly unchristian thing to say to any Christian, as it almost sounds like a threat of excommunication. But desperate men sometimes do desperate things.)

The devout Christians hear you and respond immediately. After all, they are already "in." Not so, the periphery. After a long, long time of thinking it over, the peripheral Christians finally "take the pledge"; they will no longer be peripheral. You once again have a committed church. At last, no more periphery. Or so you think!

Look again! Those folks who were formerly peripheral Christians have come in to this newly purged "company of the committed" and moved once again to the periphery!

I am telling you, dear reader, you just cannot win against these mellow folks.

I ask you again, if you have a solution, a real solution—an ethical, non-damaging, non-sectarian answer to this dilemma— please let us know!

When the Peripheral Christian Becomes the Church's Standard

The ultimate danger of the peripheral Christian comes when he sets the standard of your church.

Generally speaking, Christians who meet together outside the more traditional church are a committed people seeking to raise a new standard for the kingdom of God, to restore things lost, to know Christ, to hold high those things of great spiritual value. These people know they exist for a definite purpose and they have a burning passion.

---

* Why did I not say Methodist, Prebyterian, or Catholic? I always pick on the Baptists. I am one!

Not so the "hands-in-his-pockets" believer. Neither the dedication, nor the vision, nor the "long haul" view is there. But, like it or not, he is there! Uncommitted. Blessing-absorber. Like the poor—he is always there. And the more the Lord blesses your meetings, the more his kind appear!

What can this mellow fellow do to harm the kingdom of God? Primarily it is his influence on new Christians that is so destructive.

Please see a new Christian come into his first meeting. He has a heart for God, but he will be influenced by the standard of the other Christians in this church, of course. And who, pray tell, will he meet first? Why, those ever-friendly, peripheral Christians!

The uncommitted Christians seem to have all the time in the world to meet, and spend time with, new Christians. So the peripheral Christians' standard is the *first* standard the new Christian encounters. The "Christian life" which he sees in their lives becomes his norm. This situation can drive a Christian worker up the wall. And, yes, sometimes it drives him to do something stupid.

Ignatius Loyola is a case in point. Have you ever heard of Ignatius Loyola? He did something very foolish in his effort to keep out "the company of the lukewarm." As a result of having been fed up with the uncommitted, Ignatius Loyola started the Jesuits. Enter robes, vows, blind commitment, celibacy, fasting, sleeping on cold floors, and owning nothing. Loyola was trying to eliminate the lukewarm. Trying to solve the "problem of peripherals" is what started the whole monastic movement. They saw the same problem we see: Peripheral people drag down the very standard of the kingdom of God.

Because of the peripheral Christian, everything called "Christian" on this planet seems to eventually end up looking like a dead Baptist church. The demise of so many good intentions is rooted in the triumph of the uncommitted.

No Christian worker in his right mind wants to be like Ignatius Loyola. Nonetheless, this downward pull of the uncommitted could make you a little jealous of his idea. Of course, after a few hundred years, even in the Society of Jesus the peripheral Jesuits finally won out!

No Christian should be deprived of his right to be an ordinary human being, wear ordinary clothes, and talk in the same grammatical syntax as those around him. Certainly I am not going to join the monks, nor would I encourage you to do so.

On the other hand, those of us who are serious about the Lord and His house, who have a heart to see restoration of His house in our lifetime, are scared out of our wits at the thought of the long-term influence of the uncommitted.

The door of the church of our Lord Jesus should be open to all believers. Right? Absolutely! And yet we live daily with the influence of peripheral Christians, an eroding, corrupting influence which draws all life down to the lowest possible expression. What is a worker to do in seeking to keep the doors of the church open to all believers and at the same time keep a high standard? And, even more, a revolutionary spirit?

With that question burning in my heart, I have a word to say here to the uncommitted. What I have to say to them is the closest thing I have to a solution to the problem they create by their presence in the church.

Will you, the uncommitted, cause us to "lay down the law" in order to solve the problem you create? If we do such a thing, we end up forfeiting the very reason for which we exist! We are against rules and legalism, but if we do nothing to counter your influence, you will overwhelm us by sheer numbers. The church will end up with your low standard. When that happens we have, once again, lost our very reason for existing.

Yes, every Christian has a right to come in to a fellowship of believers. But you, the happy wanderer; you, the uncommitted; you, the critical; you, the lukewarm...ought to make up your mind. You should either make a commitment to Christ that involves the totality of your life, energies and goals, or quietly tiptoe out. You ought not to keep standing on the sidelines, warming your hands at a fire built by others through spiritual expenditure.

Look at it this way, dear peripheral Christian, there are at least forty thousand Southern Baptist churches out there that are anxious to have you as a member. Please go join one of them. But pleeeze, whatever else you do...stay away from the body of believers I meet with!

But you will not listen, will you?

You, the peripheral Christians, seem to demand the right to be lukewarm *only* in the very best, most wonderful church life experience on this planet!

This world is full of denominations and churches waiting for peripheral Christians. They are looking for you, begging for you. They would be blissfully happy to have a Christian like you, who will report in on Sunday morning, throw two dollars into the offering plate, and pass quietly out of the life of the church for the next six days! There must be at least three hundred thousand such churches in America alone. Why do you insist on being part of something new and wonderful... lukewarmly!

Now, I will say something to you in print that I cannot say to you face to face, because it is against my theological convictions to make a test of fellowship over the fact that you are a lukewarm Christian!

Here goes:

"Do not drag down the standard which was planted here, a standard planted at our birth, long before you arrived. Go somewhere else. The main purpose you now serve in the body of Christ is but that of furnishing kindling wood for a church split, and of dragging down the standard we first raised here.

"Keeping peripheral Christians out of a living experience of church life is an art none of us possess. But speaking openly, honestly, frankly, and speaking for dozens of other Christian workers outside the religious system: You have no idea how you folks thwart the kingdom of God, the house of God, the purpose of God. You have no idea what destruction you wreak in the emotional and physical life of a worker, nor the horrible pain you cause in the lives of God's people. If only every Christian minister and Christian worker could sit down with you and tell you the tragedies caused by you, the peripheral Christian! We have been trying to find a solution to the 'peripheral problem' for as long as church history has existed, and we have not found it yet. You are impenetrable."

Who could guess the overwhelming power of the mellow?

I am personally committed to raising to greater heights the very standard of past church history as it relates to church life. Not Ignatius Loyola's way, nor Assisi's way...but in the spirit of the grace of the first century. On one hand, I seek to see the church live in unity and in love, without fear, without pressure to conform and with a real sense of freedom, a church open to all believers, free of doctrinal and sectarian barriers. And I am committed to a church where there is no minister-layman distinction, and to meetings where everyone functions, shares and ministers.

On the other hand, I don't wish to end up with a bunch of sedate believers reporting in to hear a great Sunday morning sermon. Frankly, you who are the "committed lukewarm" have been messing up such high ideals as these for eighteen hundred years!

If I have to choose between the ways of Ignatius, Darby, legalism, rules, and a sectarian spirit...if I have to choose between that and being engulfed by the peripheral Christian...I will choose the latter. But be warned, dear peripheral Christian, as long as God lends me breath I mean to make it so hot for you—not legalistically, but spiritually—that you are going to have a very hard time sticking around.

Here, then, dear reader, is the problem of the mellow. And though there may be no solution, perhaps this chapter will help us to understand one of the problems we face in the diastole and systole of church unity.

One parting shot. Won't someone out there please start a denomination specifically for peripheral Christians? Look at it this way, you could almost effortlessly end up with the biggest denomination on earth!

CHAPTER 16

NON-ENEMIES
AND
NON-FRIENDS

Have you ever heard of a church having "non-friends" and "non-enemies"? Well, if you take a situation of interlocking friendships, add to that peripheral Christians, and then mix in some "non-friends" and "non-enemies," you have a brew that can kill not only a church, but even a herd of charging elephants.

Please look at the following list. See it as a chain of interlocking friendships, with the people on one end of the list not even knowing the people on the other end of the list. But also note *who* the people are at each end of this list:

THE CHURCH
The Peripherals
Semi-Friends
Almost Friends
Non-Friends
Non-Enemies
Almost Enemies
Semi-Enemies
ENEMIES!

The "peripheral" people and the "semi-friends" on one end of the list may not even know the people who are "semi-enemies" and "enemies" at the other end of the list. But even though they don't know the church's enemies, you can be sure they are close friends of everyone else on the list. Hence, the interlocking web of friendships.

It is now time for you to be introduced to the wondrous world of "almost friends" and "non-friends."

These are people who visited the church meeting once, and said, "No way am I going to get into anything where people are that serious in their commitment to Christ!" "Almost friends" and "non-friends" took one look at church life and ran for the door. They knew they were not committed, and they knew they were not going to become committed. They ran. But they didn't run far. In fact, they only got an inch or two farther out than the peripheral Christians.

These almost-friends and non-friends are the folks who drop in on your meetings about once every two months, say hello, and disappear again for weeks at a time. Then, suddenly, and for no reason, they reappear.

They never come in, but they never quite go away.

Your church's "non-friends" have a way of finding one another. They run around with one another. They become a clan. And...they are always close friends with the peripheral Christians in your church.

Let me illustrate.

One night you look up and see a host of these folks in the meeting. They are wearing big smiles and look as if they have finally joined you. Wholeheartedly! Interest seems to ooze out of every pore. "How did this happen?" you ask yourself, naively. At the end of the meeting two of these "almost friends" stand up and announce to the church that they are going to be married. They invite all of us to come to their wedding.

Need I tell you? They are looking for a ready-made crowd to attend their marriage ceremony! To them, this fellowship of believers has a big sign over it which reads: CHRISTIANS FOR RENT. FREE!

The peripheral Christians jump into the wedding preparations feet first. Do they ever get involved! They also enlist the rest of us. Before it is over, nearly everyone is working night and day to prepare for *the wedding.* And like sheep to the slaughter, we all show up at the festivities.

Guess who else is there! The church's dear and beloved non-friends have invited some other people to the wedding. Yes, all the semi-friends are there; and the almost-friends, and the peripherals, and the church. But that is not all. Also invited are the church's non-enemies, almost-enemies, semi-enemies, *and* the enemies.

After the wedding you go to the reception, sit down in a corner, sip a glass of punch, and watch. What you see is as predictable as the sunrise. Across the room you see one of those wonderful, innocent Christians who has just moved three thousand miles across America just to be part of this church's fellowship. And who is he/she talking to? *The* enemy. The two of them are getting along fabulously. This fellow who is your sworn enemy is warm, friendly, all smiles, one hundred percent Christian and a paragon of innocence. No one else knows, but you know: You are probably seeing that dear, young, innocent Christian who just moved here—for the very last time.

That is not all. Whole new interlocking webs of friendships are being formed before your very eyes. These new friendships will forever establish a no-growth situation in your church. You are seeing the death of your church...at a nice, friendly, innocent wedding!

Who did this to you? Those well meaning "almost friends" and all *their* friends!

Maybe we should not be drawn in as chair-filler-uppers for a non-friend's wedding. And maybe we should stop the enemy.

Maybe.

But who is "we"? What right do I, what right do you, what right does anybody have to tell a fellow believer not to go to a certain wedding? What kind of a human being does a thing like that to another human being?

Have you any idea how much pain you can cause a Christian by stopping him from going to someone's wedding? Or the confusion? Who gave you such a right, anyway? And have you any idea how sectarian and ugly you will cause Christians to become if you start warning them about enemies, ghosts and goblins? Or showing them that certain parties, weddings, meetings, friendships, etc. are off limits to *your* breed of Christian?

Tell Christians in the church of God not to go to a certain wedding? Dare you take such a stand? Are you mad? Stark, raving mad?

The final outcome of prohibiting a Christian from running around with another Christian will far exceed just breaking off friendship. After you have succeeded in getting your people to break off friendships, they will do more than end friendships; they will turn violently on friends, non-friends and enemies, and rage at them, "Never again will you use me like this. I never intend to speak to you again as long as I live!" It always happens that way. You see, you cannot teach people to only half-hate.

Do you wish to raise up a church whose people act like that? Do you wish me to?

No, dear Christian friend, this whole thing of division is a no-win proposition—whatever any of us do.

But don't make the bad situation of a split worse by telling your people who they can run around with and who they cannot run around with.

(On the other hand, expect disaster if you do *not* stop such things!)

One more thing you should know: If you ever try to end the maneuverings of all those non-friends and semi-friends, with their weddings, birthday parties, etc., they will scream to high heaven. They will holler across America (and throw in Europe to boot) that you are sectarian, mean, divisive, ugly and downright cruel. And while they are accusing you of causing a breakup in dear and lifelong friendships, they will in the same breath absolutely vow they are innocent of all wrongdoing.

Furthermore, they will be believed! By absolutely everyone. On both sides of the Atlantic...and throw in the Pacific. And you have not one shred of proof to the contrary. And you will be branded as an old "meany" by just about everyone. So you learn never to tangle with these people.

On the other hand, if you don't stop all those peripheral Christians, interlocking friendships, semi-friends, almost enemies, and enemies, you will see your church destroyed. That is the end result for workers who do not fight. Eventually you will find yourself sitting on a park bench in the middle of winter, muttering incoherently to yourself while throwing peanuts to pigeons that flew south months ago.

Dear Christian worker, hear me. You cannot win!

CHAPTER 17

WHAT SPLITS DO
TO WORKERS

Where does a Christian worker end up after a steady diet of splits and raids after thirty or forty years in the ministry? I do not know, but if he is still in the ministry, wherever he is, he is probably *over-reacting.*

The truth is, after a lifetime of seeing divisions, most ministers are over-reacting to the mere *possibility* of a split. True, sometimes the split he sees is not there. He is reacting to shadows! Instead of waiting until a full-blown split develops, as he did in his youth, today the weary minister may react very early to what he sees as a potential split.

On the other hand he may not be over-reacting. In stopping the problem early, he may be exercising great wisdom. Is he being wise, or over-reacting? God alone knows!

Be a little sympathetic with Christian workers for just a moment. Sometimes they do see ghosts. Yes, it is possible they might see a potential division when there really is none. Yes, and sometimes they over-react. But you cannot prove a worker is over-reacting any more than he can prove he is exercising great wisdom.

Is the minister seeing only shadows? Or does he know something you do not know? If you were seeing a situation arise which always, in the past, had ended in division every time, what would you do in that situation if you were a Christian worker?

Right now perhaps all you see in your church is a disgruntled Christian over in the corner quietly griping. (You know the kind, the professional belly-acher!) All you noted was that in a recent meeting he asked a barbed question. The minister who watched that question fly may see a split brewing. Who can tell which of you is seeing reality?

Maybe, just maybe, the minister knows a lot more about the situation than you do.

Let's say that every morning you leave the house and walk to your garage to get in your car. Once or twice a year you hear a loud popping noise; about four seconds later you are hit by a lightning bolt! Now, let's say that one morning I am watching you go to your car. There is a loud popping noise. Suddenly you run off wildly, screaming as you go. I would very definitely get the idea that you were over-reacting to a popping noise. Especially when it turns out this sound was just some firecrackers set off by a neighbor's child. Were you really over-reacting? And if you were, could anyone blame you?

Well, this is pretty much the condition a Christian worker is in after twenty or thirty years of ministry. He reacts pretty strongly to possible lightning bolts. No matter how hard he tries not to think about it, all those memories of lightning bolts, searing pain, ambulance sirens, emergency rooms and months in the hospital make him a little jumpy when he hears a popping sound!

And remember, not many Christian workers survive to middle age. An awful lot of them have either died of a direct hit from a lightning bolt, or they have reached the point that they refuse to step outside the house.

Hard to believe?

Well, Southern Baptists recently released this interesting statistic: Every day three Southern Baptist ministers quit the ministry. That statistic probably does not surprise any Christian worker over forty.

Among unstructured churches, where there are no protecting denominational walls, rituals, and no organizational structure to shield you, the number of men succumbing is just as great.

What destroys most men called of God? Discouragement born of splits heads the list.

But you know what really troubles me? It is the number of men who stay in the ministry who, after years of being caught up in divisiveness, begin living their lives in such a way as to avoid any possibility of division. Most men pull in their enthusiasm, cool their fire and simply try to minister in such a way that nothing they do or say could get them in trouble. *That* really concerns me.

Can you, therefore, be a little sympathetic with those war veterans who are still serving the Lord with a fire in their bones, bloody but unbowed? And could you possibly be just a little patient and forgiving, if occasionally such a man appears to be over-reacting to some minor church tiff? Remember, there is always that chance that the loud popping noise he hears really is a lightning bolt!

Somewhere along the way most workers do begin nipping division in the bud before it really gets serious. They have seen so much dissension that when someone begins complaining, it takes all the self control they have to keep from automatically believing the church will split...*next week!*

Combat fatigue. Occupational hazard. It's unavoidable. Such is the fate of those who are servants in the house of God. It comes with the territory!

I have been watching this "over-reacting" happen to Christian workers ever since I entered the ministry three decades ago. First as a seminary student, then as a young pastor, then as a much-traveled evangelist, I saw this reflex action taking place in so many older ministers. They were seeing and hearing things which go "bump" in the dark!

Yes, there really is a big difference between a brother in the church who is griping, or is restless, as over against a brother who is about to start a split.

Dealing with these two totally different problems calls for the greatest discernment which a man of God can find. Even then he often miscues. Breathes there a man who can tell which is which?

And if you *know* a split is coming, and you try to head it off, always remember that the Lord's people (who almost never see a split coming) will think you a terrible person for picking on some sweet, innocent saint! Everyone—I repeat, EVERYONE—thinks you are over-reacting!

Nip a division in the bud before it becomes a division, and you can never prove it was a division! The only way to really prove it will one day become a split is to let it become a split. Some choice!

Probably most men do not start out to actually cause a split. It just ends up that way. So no matter which route you take, a lot of God's people are going to get hurt.

Whatever else you do, never start a split, and never join one.

We will close this chapter with a brief look at a Christian minister who is celebrating his fortieth year in the Lord's work. This dear old beat up, chewed up brother has gone one whole month without seeing a split or a raid in the church! He takes this rare opportunity of peace to launch (at last!) the greatest dream of his Christian life. For this golden moment he has borne forty years of unbelievable abuse, persecution, etc., etc. He is about to undertake the one project for which all his life has been lived.

Now just as he launches into his fondest goal, he discovers a new split brewing. (At least, it looks exactly like all the other twenty-five splits and raids he has observed over the last forty years.)

Trust me, you can expect this dear brother to do one of the following:

(1) Shoot himself in the foot so he won't have to fight in this war! OR—

(2) Go to the edge of Bottomless Hole, grab a wild tiger in one hand, a roaring lion in the other, drink poison, set himself on fire, and leap into the pit while singing "Open up those pearly gates." OR—

(3) He might simply go stark, raving mad before he ever even reaches the cliff. You will easily recognize him. He is that man running down the street, screaming: "Oh, no! Not again—puh-leez, not again!" OR—

(4) He might throw a conniption fit. He just might order the complainers out of the church, and pass a law that never again can anyone, ever, under any conditions, gripe, gossip, sow discord, split the fellowship, or disagree with him—about anything, forever and forever, world without end. OR—

(5) Who knows, given the right circumstance, he might even over-react!

And that, dear reader, is where just about every Christian worker in the world ends up.

Light a candle for us!

CHAPTER 18

WHEN TO LEAVE

Throughout this book I have implored you not to split a group of Christians, nor to ever join a split. Fine. But one day you may feel you really must leave the church you are in. Then do so. By all means follow your conscience. But just before you leave, ask yourself a few questions. In leaving, are you following a lifelong pattern? Are you a person who gets his feelings hurt easily? Do you just naturally gravitate to controversy? Have you left several other places before? Of course these are difficult questions to answer about yourself. Who knows his own heart?

I recommend you find an excellent Christian counselor who knows neither you nor your church; sit down with him for two or three sessions and talk this over thoroughly.

Write down the reasons you are leaving. Then look at your list. Bring it to the Lord. Also write down how you are leaving. (Quietly? With a group? Full of hurt? Reconciled? Un-reconciled?)

Just to be equitable, I have chosen a few reasons *not* to leave a group. (Please consider them.) And a few good reasons very definitely to leave a group. (Please consider these, also.)

By the way, leaving a church because the preacher's sermons are boring (or because you do not like the preacher) is a pretty poor reason for leaving; nonetheless leave if you must. But to *split* a church because the sermons are boring or you don't like the preacher is an outrage! Outrage or not, it is probably the number one reason most people leave a church, and split a church! Oh, brokenness, where are you?

The second most frequent reason for leaving is probably that this whole thing called "church" is boring.

I don't even know how to address the first issue except to say that because a church or a preacher's sermons are boring is absolutely no reason to split a church. If you are going to leave for this reason, leave quietly, alone, and without comment!

As to the second, I offer my fullest sympathy. Most church services really can bore you to death. But that, too, is no reason to split a church.

What if you disagree with what your minister is teaching? Or do you believe he is "doctrinally unsound"? Dear saint of God, just what is "doctrinally unsound"? If a leader is denying that Jesus Christ is Lord, such a man is not a Christian. If a man does not believe Jesus Christ is God come in the flesh, he is not a Christian. Beyond that, every one of us on this planet disagrees with everyone else on earth about what is and what is not "doctrinally unsound."

An out-and-out denial of the Godness of either the Father, the Son, or the Holy Spirit is heresy. So also denial of the Trinity. But be careful, dear Christians; whose doctrine of the Trinity does he not believe in? Your Trinity? There must be fifteen hundred different interpretations of "what is the Trinity"! We Christians are Trinitarians. But there are endless versions of exactly what the Trinity is. In fact, there is one version for just about every believer who ever lived! Which Trinity view are you breaking fellowship with him over?

Differences of view about the Lord's coming? I have never met two men with exactly the same view on this subject. Really, now, your leaving must be for some other reason.

"I feel led of God to leave." Then leave. But I doubt a little bit that He also told you to criticize as you departed, or get angry, or take others with you. It is my studied judgment that God has never led any man to split a local gathering of God's people.

Are there good reasons to leave? Absolutely! Here are a few:

Bizarre behavior on the part of a leader.

Living in a group where everything is an "Alice in Wonderland" world, a place so surrealistic that people's minds and logic are rearranged. These are good reasons to leave.

But be careful; did you just come up with a whole new view of bizarre behavior and surrealism? One so anemic it could fit almost anyone? There have been some very eccentric men of God in church history!

Recently a brother told me stories about the group he belonged to. It appears, if what he said was true, that this was one of those groups where people are always receiving "a word from the Lord." There was a constant outpouring of predictions, confrontations, rebukes, wild assertions, demands, etc. Every day. What I said to him I would say to anyone who is in a similar situation: "If what you are telling me is true, then this group is mad. And you are mad if you stay!"

If the group you are in is truly bizarre, I would say the same to you. Unfortunately, ninety-nine percent of the time Christians belong to groups in which things are not that black and white. In virtually all situations, you are dealing with grays, never blacks and whites.

What about all these groups which claim to be special? They claim to be *the* move of God, to be "it"! For a Christian who really believes he belongs to that special, select group to one day wake up and discover he must leave is one of the worst traumas a soul can face. The question haunting him is, "Leave God's work on this earth? Is that true? If it is God's work, dare I leave?" This dilemma can destroy a Christian. It has already destroyed thousands of Christians in dozens of such "elitist" groups.

And it does not get any easier when all his friends tell him that if he leaves he will surely reap damnation.

If a leader is teaching *"This church is God's work in this age,"* and adding, *"If you leave, God is finished with you,"* (1) that leader ought to be ashamed of himself; (2) he ought to get some professional counseling; or (3) he should quit the ministry; (4) or, better, all of the above! Such talk on the part of a leader (or a church) is a sign of unstable mental health. Certainly it is a sign that the Lord is not central and the engine of this movement is not primarily the Holy Spirit, but, rather, it is the energy of the *soul* which is empowering that movement. To make a claim like that and also claim that Jesus Christ is central to that group is a contradiction in terms.

A word of advice: If you ever get that kind of counsel from the church you are in, pack and leave. Run! Repeat: Do not walk. Run!

If you belong to a group that tells you something terrible will happen to you if you leave, tell them you have my permission to go. If they ask whose permission, if you cannot think up a good name to give them, tell them Gene Edwards gave you permission! And if they ask what the evidence of my authority is, why tell them I have given lots and lots of people permission to leave such groups and God has not abandoned a single one of them!

Then run like crazy!

My feeling is that during the whole period surrounding a split our conduct is being watched by God and angels. Maybe not even our *inward* feelings. Maybe just our *outward* words and actions. We cannot always control how we feel inside, but our outward conduct—this we can control.

So guard your words, and rein in your conduct. Take no sides. Keep your mouth closed. Do nothing, say nothing. Wait until the whole episode is over. Wait. And then what? Then do more of the same! If you feel you must leave, do so. And wait on your God.

One day you will be pleasantly surprised to see your Lord again. He will appear just about where you last saw Him, and you will notice that His general direction is still *forward.*

CHAPTER 19

THE FEAR OF LEAVING

Many a Christian, having reached the point where he knows he cannot stay, does not leave. He is too afraid to leave.

He cannot stay, he cannot go. If he stays he will have to make some major, perhaps dangerous, change in his basic psychological nature. He will have to violate his own conscience. He will begin to conform to things that are against all his basic instincts. For health's sake if for no other reason, he might be wise to go.

Regardless of what Christian group you belong to, dear reader, you must keep your individual uniqueness. Compromising the very disposition which God gave you in your mother's womb, in order to remain in a group, is damaging not only to your body, but to your soul and to your spirit.

True, in becoming part of any group, each of us must sacrifice a little of our individuality. But there is a limit to conformity. Individuality and freedom are not non-Christian words. Individuality may be the bane of unity in some groups, but extreme conformity is the bane of good physical and mental health!

Extreme individuality produces much division. Extreme conformity destroys lives. In a church where everyone is encouraged to keep his individuality, the words of a prime minister of France keep coming to mind: "I am the prime minister of fifty million prime ministers!" Nonetheless, as difficult and dangerous as both individuality and corporateness may be, I would implore Christian workers not to create an atmosphere where people's innate dispositions bow to extreme group conformity.

Individual personality, unique disposition, and the taking of personal responsibility for making your own decisions—these do not cease when you become part of the church.

If you are afraid to leave a church even when your instincts tell you to, you need to ask yourself a few questions. Here are two for starters: (1) Do you belong to a group that is keeping you by telling you fear stories? (2) Are you fearful that God will in some way "destroy" you if you leave? (3) Are you going against your best internal judgment in staying?

If your answer is "yes" to the above, I strongly recommend you leave.

I suppose I receive more mail from Christians who have been hurt by division than any other man in America. (This is a guess.) Perhaps the most common theme running through these letters is people telling how they reached the point of leaving, but felt that God would not love them anymore if they left. Or that the Lord would punish them for leaving. Their heads were full of fear stories they had heard over and over.

"You are leaving God if you leave these people." "There is no other place on this earth for you to go." "You are rebellious." "This act is worse than witchcraft." "You are outside the headship of God." "Refuse to submit to the elders and you are in rebellion against God."

If this kind of talk really gets into your head, it can become a self-fulfilling prophecy.

Actually, you are fearful for good reason. Not because God may do something terrible to you, but because someone has been tampering with you head!

Friend, this prophecy of doom will always collapse. In any group. Anywhere. In any age.

Let me illustrate.

If you are now in a group declaring, "We are going further, things are being done and said and experienced which have never before been done and said," and if that statement is absolutely correct, even while this is being said, God is out there preparing a better man, and a better work! Somewhere! Or at that very moment your Lord may be laying His hand on a young man whom *they* just excommunicated last week.

There is no man (and no movement) that cannot be trumped. That is the way of God.

And to you, dear Christian worker, who allow these fear stories to spread in your church, and to you who claim no one can leave your church and keep God's full blessing, a little humility on your part might save some of your people from great damage!

There are probably no more than a dozen men during any hundred-year period who do accomplish truly pioneering work. One of these special men is out there right now, being raised up by God, who will trump everything done before. Bow low, dear brother; the days *your* movement is "it" are few in number, if any at all.

I would like to pause here and say a straight word to Christian workers who are in movements that claim, "Our church is special," and those who claim, "If you leave us, God is through with you," *and* those of you who tell horror stories about people who have left your group.

You, sir, are hurting Christians. You are—or will be— destroying many Christians with such talk. But perhaps even more, you are damaging the cause of Christ. Throughout the last seventeen centuries there have always been wonderful groups standing outside tradition; they have left us with an important testimony of Christ and His church. The lives and testimony of those faithful soldiers are a great encouragement to all future generations. But in our generation some of you have introduced something into this ancient and venerable saga which has never been there before. You bring shame on the name of all those gallant souls of the last seventeen hundred years. Those people were very special people. History has testified to their significance. But they never claimed to be special. You cannot find them saying that they were God's only, exclusive, chosen work on this earth.

But you do! For shame. You have no business claiming to be that which only a verdict of history can make you. Consider this, too. Other ministers inside (and outside) the traditional churches stand horrified at your claims. You do not serve the cause of Christ by your boast, either within or without the structured church. Furthermore, it is going to be very hard for history to lay a wreath of honor at your grave, knowing that a large part of the unction, drive and enthusiasm of your movement came from an appeal to people's ego! Finally, you are making the task of restoration harder for the generations to come.

Angels do not know what is or is not God's work in this age. How can you know?

Dear Christian worker, such talk is not necessary to accomplish your mission. If you cannot grow in number and draw men to Christ without this elitist talk, you might rethink just how much you really have to offer. Might I also recommend that you locate the seminary nearest you and enroll in a few courses in ministerial ethics!

But what of you dear Christians who are in such churches? You may truly be in the greatest thing that ever existed, and you may be blissfully happy there. Nonetheless, you *must never be afraid* to leave a group that makes outrageous claims that something terrible will happen to you if you leave.

True leadership, ethical leadership, does not need such talk in order to carry on the work of God.

There is this joyful hope that perhaps a day will come when people will be raised up by God who present only Christ, claim nothing, and end up doing a better work than anyone else ever has.

I close by saying this to those of you who think you may be in an unethical group as I have described: Regardless of how negative you feel toward this group, you still have no business splitting it! The only ethical thing you can do is quietly leave. Without fear.

CHAPTER 20

PREVENTIVE MAINTENANCE*

What can I do to foster an atmosphere in my fellowship that will minimize the possibility of damaging a child of God? What can you do in the local body of believers to which you belong? What can the church as a whole do? Preventing a division is impossible short of throwing your whole church in a jail, but minimizing the hurtful fallout is not impossibility.

May I suggest a few possibilities?†

The church is to be a positive thing in the lives of Christians, doing more to build a Christian than to destroy him. Yet there are many deeply damaged brothers and sisters; therefore there

---

† As you give thought to how to execute preventive mainten-ance in your church, one thing you can do is have your people do some reading on the subject of church splits. That, of course, is the purpose of this book. See the last page for other references.

should be help available within the church to minister to that damage. A highly skilled Christian counselor would go a long way toward addressing this need.

From time to time, in every assembly of believers, there are those who feel they must leave that church and go somewhere else. This decision to leave should be an occasion for acceptance and support by every member of that local body. We ought to be there, to help such people pack and to send them off with a warm good-bye and a royal invitation to return.

Lines of communication in the church must be open...for all...to all. There are dozens of ways to do this. One way *not* to do it is for major church decisions to be made behind closed doors by "elders" with only the final outcome being made known to everyone else.

Certainly the private life and personal decisions of God's people should not be interfered with unless assistance is voluntarily requested. Even then, guidance should only be suggested, and that with great prudence. Neither you, nor I, nor any other person or group of persons in the church has any business telling anyone how to live their private lives. Our individual characteristics, attitudes, lifestyles, and dispositions should be honored and respected.

Some other suggestions.

Everything the church does should come about in such a way that it leads to wholeness in the body of Christ.

There should be a moderated view of all things—except Christ Himself.

The atmosphere of the church should contribute to a healthy mental and emotional state in all our lives.

Sectarianism and exclusivism stand at the door of every church, very near to getting in. They are there *right* now. Addressing that fact with a view of preventing exclusivism and elitism is a sign of security and wholeness.

Religious nuttiness, fanaticism and screwballism in general have no place in the house of God.

Everything we emphasize should be seasonal. Go to seed on nothing.

Nothing should be emphasized out of proportion to other parts of the Christian faith; nothing should be emphasized for long periods of time.

We need to foster the attitude that "we" ("our little church," or "our movement," or "our denomination") are not God's gift to mankind, nor the best and final work of God, nor are we the final and sole repository of all truth. There are almost certainly some other people out there, people whom we have never heard of, who are *better* at doing anything and everything we do!

When trouble arises, each of us needs to have already been schooled in preserving unity and in seeking to move heaven and earth not to hurt another Christian.

* * *

Now, can a church so order its life and so express the Lord Jesus Christ that many of the matters just mentioned can become a living reality in the lives of the members of that body?

Well, here are a few practical possibilities based upon actual experience which you might wish to consider.

First of all, how can we deal with the potential danger of sectarian attitudes in our midst?

Here is one to chew on. In recent years we have been encouraging everyone in our gathering to take off from six months to a year after the first three years of being here. Why? Just so a believer can have time to see if church life is really what he/she wants, and so that everyone can have a good, long opportunity to "look around," visit and experience other kinds

119

of church expression. A family taking a whole year away from church—what a wholesome way to decide if *this* really is the place you wish to be! I dare you to encourage that in your gathering!

It is a standing feature of our gathering that everyone take one to two months off from the meetings, *every* year. Why? Well, we all have our entire lifetime to be Christians; taking time out every year from what we fondly call "church life" is an effective way to prevent spiritual and ecclesia burnout.

Next, I would urge any Christian to take a sabbatical (that is, take off one year in seven) from any dynamic Christian movement. Why? For the sake of health of the body, soul and spirit. And during that year I would recommend you visit all sorts of other expressions of the church. I have an idea that if some churches and movements followed the above advice they would probably lose most of their membership. If you can only keep your people by means of walls, fences, group pressure and out-and-out brainwashing, you really do not have much, do you? If you have something substantial to offer God's people, why be afraid to encourage them to test out that fact?

We have present in our gathering a trained Christian counselor. He keeps a Biblically-based, Christ-centered counseling program alive among us. Counseling is led by a brother who (1) has lived virtually his entire adult Christian life in church life and (2) holds a master's degree in Christian marriage and family counseling. This brother is also responsible for the church having or giving training in premarital counseling, preventive maintenance in marriage, counsel for singles, etc.

Why a counselor? Well, because at one time or another every marriage needs an impartial, outside referee, that's why. And every unmarried man or woman needs someone wise to talk to.

Nor is a counselor where we stop. There are at least half dozen other (older) Christians present in the body who are available to help anyone with a problem. Night or day. Free.

We also have some very special people in our midst! These folks are unique in this world. I will call them anti-sectarian storm troopers. They are all a little older and wiser than most of the people in our gatherings. These are people experienced in (1) church life and in (2) watching out for quirky Christians.

Here is what they may do. At the slightest sign of (1) spiritual overload, (2) overzealous commitment, (3) a sectarian attitude that "we are it", (4) the merest sign someone among us is thinking of doing a little sheep-stealing from some other group, or (5) any other signs of religious fanaticism, there are these people—mature Christians if you please—who are ready, willing and able to urge that brother or sister to back off and seek a balanced perspective on life in general, and the church in particular.

May their tribe increase.

Everything we do in our experience of church life is done in such a way as to preserve a balanced atmosphere among God's people. We seek to do nothing that would cause anyone to begin developing a sectarian attitude.

Frankly, when a brother exhibits a sectarian attitude on his own (without having ever been trained to be sectarian by the group he is in), it is my studied judgment that he is showing signs of psychological instability. Sectarianism is not native to a well-balanced Christian.

A sectarian, denominating (or any kind of exclusivist or "we-are-special") attitude is either acquired from outside influences or as a result of some kind of internal psychological problem.

Put that in your cud and chew on it!

Of the brothers I work with, not one has ever divided anything. They have never engaged in any kind of ugly scene with other Christians, inside or outside the church. Nor have they ever stopped a potential split nor scotched a raid.

And if any future Christian workers come out of our midst, it is my hope they will maintain that record.

Unfortunately there are few workers on this earth with such a track record. Those who have such a track record hold my undying admiration. Fighting, raising a stink, going on the offensive would be so much easier. To die is hard. The worker who lays down his life in the presence of division is a rare man, indeed. From such dying, tears, and broken hearts comes a testimony which, if nothing else, gives to me and to other Christian workers strength and encouragement on rainy days.

Dear Christians, do not break the hearts of this rare breed of worker by devastating their lives—or the body of Christ—by participation in division. And if that is not motive enough, then consider this before you become party to a split or a raid: Remember what it does to the heart of God.

We could go on with a much longer list of practical things to do to maintain a healthy atmosphere and open lines of communication in a church, but I would close with one I have already mentioned.

It is the way you say good-bye. It is my judgement that you can learn a lot about a church from the way it says good-bye to those Christians who feel they need to belong somewhere else. I realize that saying good-bye with true Christian charity to someone who sets off ten tons of TNT before leaving may be downright impossible. But what of the simple Christian who, causing no problems, needs to move on somewhere else?

Every grace of helpfulness and encouragement should be extended to such a one departing your midst. He should feel more than welcome to return for a visit, or to return again permanently. No atmosphere should ever be created in a church that prevents a people from extending a simple, helpful goodbye to those who leave. Let an atmosphere of such charity be the goal of your church.

A last word in closing this chapter. One of the best things a church can do to prevent division (heresy of heresies!) is to have lots of fun!

CHAPTER 21

WHERE IS GOD IN ALL THIS?

Splits

Division

Ugliness

Claims

Counter-claims

Devastation

WHERE IS GOD IN ALL THIS?

My wife Helen was in a meeting in which a very wise man was asked about splits. The question was, "Which side did God take in all that?" The answer, wisely given, was, "The Lord takes His own side."

Where is the Lord in the midst of this carnage? The Lord does not take sides. Methinks He may have no opinions about splits. He may just be watching *sheep.*

What? A non-denominating God? Perish the thought!

All those Christians threatening one another with everlasting damnation are His children. They are all God's children.

The fight, supposedly, is over theology and, of course, your side is right. But here is a non-theological God watching. I do not think He is all that impressed with the theology of any Christian, especially when that theology destroys other Christians. Nor is He all that impressed with our views. Nor our claims. Nor who is right. Nor even who is wrong! There are at least ten thousand good theologies on the face of the earth, and every one of them believes nine thousand nine hundred and ninety-nine other theologies are wrong.

Where does God stand?

I think He stands back. Way back. And watches. Hoping that somewhere in all this carnage there will be one heart that will survive the holocaust and be able to come back and fully, freely, fervently love Him again.

I hope you are that one.

CHAPTER 22

DIVISION, THE CHILD
OF FREEDOM

I would like to address a very special kind of Christian in this chapter. I write to those of you who meet in homes, not in church buildings. If you are in a more institutional-type church, this chapter will not pertain to you, and you probably will not identify with a lot of what is said. Nonetheless you are welcome to "peek" into this little world if you wish.

Splits in informal church gatherings occur just as often as in traditional-type churches. Why so much division in a place where you would suppose division to be almost non-existent?

The answer? There is more freedom and openness out here in informal churches, and that is especially true of the meetings.

In church life everyone knows everyone else; there is devotion to Christ and to one another which goes far beyond the traditional practice of "punching in on Sunday at eleven and punching out at noon." But one of the crucial differences lies in our meetings. Everyone participates, speaking, sharing, etc. In such an atmosphere some also give an opinion. This chance to present one's opinion feels so new and refreshing that it can get out of hand. For some this offering of an opinion does not stop after the meeting is over. Nor is the opinion always positive.

Step back and look at an open meeting. What you see is a lot of activity, sharing, yes, and even opinionizing, all occurring in an atmosphere that is free of structure and ritual. There are enough ingredients in that mixture, dear reader, to keep a church sitting on a stack of dynamite for the rest of its life.

Frankly, I am always amazed at the lightning-fast transition which a Christian makes when coming out of the institutional church and into a free-flowing expression of church life found in home gatherings. All his life this fellow has been checking in at eleven on Sunday morning, never uttering a word, never offering an opinion, never *having* an opinion; lo and behold, after only one week in a non-structured atmosphere he is trying to run the whole church!

(Weep here.)

I reflect back on my time as a Baptist pastor. Everything in our Sunday morning church services was prearranged. Fifty years before I got there! There wasn't room in one of those services for so much as a peep. This approach to "church" has its definite advantages. Never sell short the advantages of structure, ritual and form. It is a work of genius when it comes to keeping out discussion!

If the Baptist church I grew up in (1) suddenly lost their pastor, (2) did away with all Sunday morning ritual, (3) gave everyone an opportunity to share; and if, at the same time, (4) the people began spending more time with one another and meeting in the informal setting of living rooms, that Baptist Church would split into more pieces than there are people!

Dominating people, cliques, grudges, and rivalries would erupt and splatter all over town.

The freedom which comes with non-structured church life is an open invitation to splits. So, what can we do to prevent such things from happening? Here are a few possibilities: End the informality; give up the freedom; introduce ritual. Here are some more: Introduce rules; run the church through a closed hierarchy; replace freedom with legalism.

Why not do that? Because that is what we came out of. Personally I would rather court disaster!

The real question is not, "How shall we stop this problem of division in an informal church setting?" The central question is, "Are you going to *follow* someone when dissension sets in? What are you going to do when ideas, opinions and criticisms begin to flourish?" There is a man who will split a church out there. Will you be one who joins the circle of dissent?

Consider the following, please, if you are part of a fellowship of believers which is operating with open meetings and a free atmosphere.

Please leave your psychoses at home. The other saints gathered there are neither your enemies, nor are they there to be your followers. Please come and join in for, say, a year. While part of this group, take this time in your life to learn the cross, learn to live in close quarters with others and, in so doing, discover that you, too, have weaknesses. By the way, those weaknesses will be found out just by living in close proximity with others. Your reaction to being "found out" will speak volumes about you. Hopefully you will allow the weaknesses in your own life to be dealt with. Learn to take your disposition, weaknesses and opinions to the cross!

Those are good words, but you can be sure someone will manage to circumnavigate all of the above. What will you do if he starts a split in the church? My answer to that question may surprise you: "Step back and let him split it!" Frankly, I have never found any other honorable way, nor *Christian* way, to deal with a split.

But here is a better question: "When that someone does inevitably start to split your church, are you going to be dumb enough to follow him?"

As we close I would like to take a look at one last, unusual, reason for splits in church life.

In the world of the informal church you will find believers who are excited, expectant, and involved, wrapped up in the Lord, His house, His people. At some point that black-hearted nature which seems to be in all of us begins expressing itself in someone. This "someone" starts to guide and direct this wonderful community of believers. Not much, mind you, just a teeny-itsy-bitty bit, and only so as to keep it from straying off its wonderful course, mind you.

It so happens that when a dozen people all want to direct this venture (just a teeny-itsy-bitty bit, so it will not get off its wonderful course), the fellowship is suddenly faced with a dozen different courses plotted by a dozen different navigators, each of whom is prepared to immolate the whole church if anyone dare use any map but his!

For that reason, expect splits to occur as much in the life of believers outside the traditional churches as in them.

There is an obvious cure for this problem, of course. I have reiterated it throughout this book, and I close by stating it again. There is one way to prevent a church split. *Never* become involved in one.

PART II

CONFLICT AND RESOLUTION
IN THE CHURCH
AS VIEWED BY A
CHRISTIAN LAWYER
by Tom Brandon

CHAPTER 23

DEALING WITH CONFLICT

The church is not prepared for conflict. Christians can't believe it will happen, we have no idea where conflict comes from, nor how to deal with it. We Christians simply do not know how to respond to conflict as the Lord might.

The church tends to vacillate between two extremes in deciding this issue. The first extreme is the refusal to admit that Christians can and do have conflicts. At the other end of the scale is the tendency to label all conflict as arising from sin on the part of the individuals involved. No doubt most conflict does have its roots in sin. However, we must note that some conflict is simply inevitable, and is not inherently sinful.

Take, for example, the dispute between Paul and Barnabas concerning John Mark. Who was in sin for causing the conflict? The Bible does not indict sin in this conflict.

But ultimately, the reason for the conflict. is really not the issue. What is of utmost importance is our response to the conflict once it arises.

We can respond from the depths of our fallen human nature, or we can respond on a "supernatural" level, from our spirits. Encouraging a church split which will result in Christian carnage is not a supernatural response. Yes, maybe some churches need to split. However, that is a decision for the Lord to make, not you.

The following chapters will attempt to view this problem of church crises and see just how deep and widespread the problem is. Then let us look at some practical ways to prevent a split, and how to deal with one (1) in the spirit, or, God forbid, (2) in the flesh!

CHAPTER 24

THE DIFFICULTY OF
RECONCILIATION

Just how big is this problem of church conflict? Just what are the chances, typically, of heading off a crisis? How interested are most Christians in reconciling with their "enemies"?

In my years of dealing with disputes within churches and among fellow believers, I have noticed that probably as many as ninety-five percent of Christians do not truly desire to be obedient to Scripture or to follow the example of the life of Jesus Christ. While many of these would feign obedience, their obedience is actually selective. In other words, they select which passages have relevance to them and their lives; they set themselves up as the final arbiters of which Scriptures should be obeyed. The other five percent, while certainly not perfect, are generally headed in the right direction in conduct and motive.

Let me share with you an observation I have made in disputes and conflicts where I have been asked to render assistance.

In no fewer than fifty percent of the cases one side has said, in essence, "We see ourselves as God's right hand of vengeance. It is our duty to inflict God's wrath in accordance with His word." An appropriate translation: "I want revenge!"

I have also observed that from the first step (when both parties sit down to talk) on to the next step of coming to grips with the issue, on to the third step, a time of seeking the Lord, and finally to the last step of reconciliation, the number of those who stay with the process steadily becomes smaller. Only a handful ever stick it out to reconciliation. Obviously a whole new mindset needs to develop across Christendom about conflict and reconciliation. The process of sitting down and talking with fellow brothers and sisters in Christ about a problem really weeds out those who are unwilling to pursue the goal of healing and unity. In these disputes, probably less than five percent ever end up with some measure of reconciliation between the parties.

It seems we have to go through a lot of desert before we find an oasis. Up until now most Christians have preferred not to make the journey. This attitude desperately needs to change.

Let me illustrate again how uncharitable churches can become, and how far reconciliation is from their minds. In one case, a church rather swiftly terminated their relationship with their senior pastor, graciously gave him two weeks severance pay, and kicked him out of the church parsonage. Later he found it very difficult to locate a job in the secular world or in his denomination. From all this he bore some deep scars. When we were contacted about this situation, we talked to the church leaders about dealing with the issues and about trying to determine whether or not there could be a reconciliation. Healing was needed, and being reconciled to one another was the key to the healing.

The comment I received from the chairman of the deacons was, "There is no way we are going to call that guy back as our pastor." I explained that the issue was not whether the man should or should not be their pastor. The issue was to rebuild relationships and to deal with the scars, the loss of reputation, and the hurt engendered by this separation. (As well as dealing with the corporate sin of the body?) Needless to say the deacons were not interested in pursuing the matter any further. They felt they were right in what they had done and that the consequences that the pastor was now suffering were brought on by himself. Today that man is no longer in the ministry. As he told me, "The hurt was too deep and the rejection too real to ever face that again." Of course the biggest struggle in his life is his struggle with bitterness. That same struggle, probably magnified, also continues in the hearts of his wife and three children.

The church that kicked him out certainly appears to have committed a wrong against a brother due to their corporate failure in handling the situation. That sin will probably stay with the congregation, and plague them, until they confess it and deal with it.

I strongly believe the body of Christ, as a local congregation, has to deal with sin in the same manner that individuals have to deal with it! They must confess it, ask for forgiveness, seek reconciliation and, where necessary, make restitution. Otherwise it appears that the church will continue to suffer from that wrongdoing until it is made right.

Consider this rather discouraging sight: A people reach an agreement and experience reconciliation, then the whole thing falls apart. What happens is that we rejoice in the resolution of the matter, pray and thank the Lord, and go our separate ways. Within a few months the vast majority of those reconciliations fall through. In fact, my experience is that up to eighty percent of the "reconciliations" fall apart.

I trust you are becoming aware that we are faced here with no small problem. The reason reconciliations fall apart is that the conflict was resolved on the soulish level, not in the spirit.

I have made a decision that life is too short to spend it trying to help Christians resolve disputes in a Biblical manner in a situation where no one is willing to do what the Bible says. My ministry is to those who are willing to pursue a scriptural, charitable, Christian path in these situations.

We, as individuals, are made up of three parts: our spirit, our soul (which is our mind, will and emotions), and our body. Most of the conflict resolution or peacemaking attempts between individuals or churches involve something in the soulish realm of our lives. They involve our mind, or our will, or our emotions. I can guarantee you, from my experience, that if a conflict is resolved on the soul level, you will have to work very hard to maintain the resolution, and occasionally patch it up, to keep everybody happy and to call it "a success."

Truly resolving conflict is the process by which we move from the fleshly or the soulish realm into the realm of the spirit. There is not, and never will be, any conflict with the Trinity or in the Trinity. Nor does the Holy Spirit tell different messages to different people. Thus, the real agony of resolving conflict is the process of eliminating any thoughts, designs, or intents from the decision or dispute which reflect the flesh or soul life of man as opposed to the spirit life. Any resolution of a dispute apart from the spirit life amounts to a compromise, a negotiated settlement, a cease-fire, or a best guess. Using man's logic to replace God's thoughts is a poor replacement for spiritual reconciliation! To move past the flesh or soul life involves a death — a death to the way we want to solve a conflict or deal with an issue. In other words, the cross. It seems to me that conflict cannot be resolved in the spirit until we first visit the cross.

CHAPTER 25

AN OUNCE OF PREVENTION

What do we do to prevent a church split? The first and most obvious answer to that question is to practice preventive maintenance prior to a crisis or split. That can be done in three different steps.

1. Inform the body about conflict in general and how it should be resolved within the corporate body and between individuals.

2. Update the church organizational and operational documents if you happen to have these to contain clear definitions on how the body will handle irresolvable disputes in the body. These documents need not be formal but should give guidance in procedure.

3. Obtain commitment from the church as a whole, as well as from individuals, to follow these guidelines on how church fights or disputes, including disputes among individual members of the body, will be handled.

As I have talked to seminary professors all across the country, they have confirmed that there is not one evangelical seminary in the United States that teaches its ministers how to resolve conflict from a Biblical perspective. Perhaps this is another place we need to see preventive maintenance inaugurated.

There are courses on how to manage conflict, but none on how to resolve disputes within the body of Christ. We are not speaking here of winning; we are addressing the possibility of godly Christian resolution to conflict. As any pastor will tell you, that is probably one of the most urgent subjects to be addressed in churches and ministry.

One of the first things a pastor is hit with upon graduating from seminary and arriving at his first church is conflict. We do not do any favors to our young ministers when we send them out full of enthusiasm and godly fervor, only to be hit in the face with a monumental dispute over what color the carpet should be. Or more importantly, why we should not carpet the floor at all because Aunt Bessie donated the beautiful wood for the floor.

While churches are playing games with numbers, as to both members and finances, there are many in the ministry who are giving up and leaving the "full-time" ministry. In fact, in the largest Protestant denomination in the United States, between a thousand and fifteen hundred of its pastors are leaving the ministry each year.

If it is too late or impossible to accomplish any or all of the three steps mentioned above and the dispute is upon you, then the most crucial thing that you can do is determine in advance what your response will be to a church crisis. If your response is to drink the bitter cup and wait on God, then you can expect to drink it alone and probably wait for a long time. Any part you play in aiding a division (while it can always be justified) is never appropriate.

CHAPTER 26

HOW TO RESPOND

When a conflict arises, what should we do? Whatever we do, it will be on the level of the spirit, or the soul, or the flesh. Let us look at the spiritual way first.

The Supernatural Response

Conflict and criticism can be compared to the ordeal that a Hebrew woman had to endure in Numbers 5. The woman had to go through a purification test if her husband felt the least bit suspicious of her faithfulness to him. It mattered not if the accusation was totally undeserved; she had to take the test.

Whenever we are criticized, or caught up in conflicting relationships, we pretty well go through this same test...even though it is completely undeserved.

It is your response in these times that will determine exactly what you are made of.

Just as the wife of a jealous husband had to drink the cup of bitter water mixed with dirt and blood taken from the floor beneath the altar, so you must drink the cup of bitter water that is handed to you in this time of crisis. You will remember that the woman in Numbers 5 had no right to defend herself or to offer any charges against the husband. It would be the Lord who vindicated her.

Your response should be to drink the cup that is given to you. Drink it all. And wait.

In my years of dealing with churches and parachurch ministries, I only know of one or two individuals (leaders) who would lay their ministry down and walk away from it. Yet I strongly recommend that you consider walking away from the church or the ministry, as the case may be.

Recently, in one church fight where I was consulted by the pastor as to what should be done, and where lines had already been drawn and sides were chosen, I offered this suggestion: Throw a party! Does not James 1:2 tell us to *consider it all joy?* My advice was that they should invite everyone in the church to a festive party celebrating the fact that the body now had a trial or tribulation in which it could rejoice. The purpose of my suggestion was to allow everyone an opportunity to focus upon the Lord and take their eyes off of each other and the conflict. The pastor thought my suggestion a novel idea, but decided that this was too serious to treat so flippantly. But was it?

One thing you *can* do is *count it joy*.

The Natural Response

A church split is as easy as pie.

Let us describe how you and your friends can help bring about a church split in one easy lesson. Just follow these simple instructions. (If you want to save a little time, skip down to the recipe located at the end of this chapter.)

142

A dispute begins developing in the congregation. This is the time to begin. Make sure the issue is important and soul-stirring. It could be over the color of the carpet in the auditorium, calling a new pastor, getting rid of one, or about a staff member who may or may not be guilty of immorality. Whatever you are capable of imagining has almost certainly caused a church split somewhere in church history.

What should be the immediate response of the congregation towards the conflict and the offender? Why, it should be outrage, judgment, righteous indignation shouldn't it? The stirring of our souls to the point that, as our duty before God, we must take a stand against sin in the camp and help God purify the Bride. Right? The quicker, the better. God talks a lot about swift justice, doesn't He?

At that point battle lines need to be drawn and the congregation divided into two camps. Everyone will fit into one camp or the other. In fact, if someone chooses not to take sides, *be highly suspicious.* Remember Jesus' words, "He who is not for Me is against Me." If someone does not choose sides, then he should be considered an enemy.

The next thing to do is plan a battle strategy. How do we defend against a takeover? Who will support us or vote with us? Or how can we control the church so that God gets back in the picture? After all, this is *God's* church. If God gave us the vision, then we must be good stewards and be faithful to what He has shown us. Right? If this is God's work, why should we let people get in the way?

All the time that strategy is being planned, someone should continue to motivate the troops with sordid accounts of what has happened. Include all the gory details that you can find or speculate about.

This last point is important. If people are not reminded of the events, they might lose interest and not participate in any big vote that might have to come up. If you can form some sort of prayer chain it would be a good way to keep important, informative rumors flowing to the troops. Prayer can really be used to your advantage. If you are in a meeting where a dispute breaks out, suggest that everyone stop and pray. It will knock the wind right out of your opponent's sails. This is especially effective if you are losing an argument.

Meanwhile, be prepared for and expect the worst from the other side. Especially during church service. Remember, do not compromise. God does not compromise with sin, does He? Whatever you say may be taken out of context by the other side and used against you, so be careful what you say. Be prepared with Scriptures and arguments to defend your position at any time. Does not Peter say in one of his epistles that we must always be ready to make a defense?

There are several techniques you can use until the big confrontation. Quote lots of Scripture; pray loud and long. Pray for God to intervene and bring peace, and to convict "them" of sin.

Don't forget the best one, "This is demonic. They are of the devil."

You have now come to the time when truth must prevail. Since you are on the side of truth, you know which side will win. What should you do? Go for the jugular! If you have to use the secular court system to enforce your rights, then do so. Truth must win at any cost.

After truth wins out, there will be a time of "sifting." Those who promoted the wrong side will usually leave. Those who were not courageous enough to be on the side of truth (the wimps) will probably also leave.

If for some reason (probably the devil) you lose the big showdown and the other side wins, be consoled that God will probably punish them for years.

A Quick Recipe for a Church Split:

Take two good rumors, add a little spice, beat in several old accusations, pour in several dissatisfied church members, season to taste and then beat until firm. Spread out the mixture as far as possible throughout the church (the fact that it is thin is okay). Bake at a high temperature until you think it is done. Serve when ready!

THE POSTPONED WEDDING

The wedding guests have gathered in great anticipation; the ceremony to be performed today has long been awaited.

The orchestra begins to play the wedding march, and the choir rises in proper precision. The bridegroom and his assistants gather in front of the chancel. One little saint, her flowered hat bobbing, leans to her companion and whispers, "Isn't he handsome?" The response is agreement, "My, yes. The handsomest..."

The sound of the organ rises, a joyous announcement that the bride is coming. Everyone stands and strains to get a glimpse of the beautiful bride.

A horrible gasp explodes from the congregation. In stumbles the bride. She is limping on one leg, wedding garment tattered and muddy; the rents in her dress leave her less than modest. Her nose is bloody, an eye is swollen. Her hair is a mess and some of it seems to have been pulled out.

The organist, fumbling over the keys, begins the march again while the attendants cast down their eyes. The congregation releases a quiet groan.

Surely the groom deserved better than this, is the thought in every mind. That handsome groom who has kept himself faithful to his love surely deserves to find consummation with the most beautiful of women—not this.

Alas, His bride, the church, has been fighting again.

[Taken from *The Key to a Loving Heart*, by Karen Mains. Published by David C. Cook, 1979.]

We would refer readers to two excellent books put out by Tyndale House Publishers. One is entitled *Tell It to the Church*, involving reconciliation, mediation and arbitration of disputes between Christians. The other volume is *Church Discipline and the Courts*, which deals with both the legal and scriptural aspects of church discipline and how they should be implemented. Also, of course, *In The Face Of A Church Split*, *Here Is Our Mission*, and *A Tale Of Three Kings*, Published by Christian Books Publishing House.

THE DEEPER CHRISTIAN LIFE

ARE YOU INTERESTED IN READING MORE ABOUT THE DEEPER CHRISTIAN LIFE?

If you are, let us suggest the order in which to read the following books, all of which have been written on the deep aspects of the Christian life.

By all means, begin with *The Divine Romance.* Then we recommend *Experiencing the Depths of Jesus Christ* and *Practicing His Presence.* Follow that with *Final Steps in Christian Maturity* and *The Inward Journey.*

For a study in brokenness, read *A Tale of Three Kings,* a favorite with thousands of believers all over the world.

The book entitled *The Spiritual Guide, Letters of Mme. Guyon* and *Letters of Fenelon,* all help to solidify, expand and buttress the things you will have read in the previous books.

ARE YOU INTERESTED IN CHURCH LIFE?

Many Christians are interested in the *vessel* which is to contain the deeper Christian life...that is, the experience of church life.

If you are one of these, perhaps you should read *"A Coming Revolution Called...Church Life."* In it Gene Edwards challenges the lay Christian and minister alike to set aside many of the present day practices of the church and to respond to the growing host of believers who are seeking a living, vital experience of church life.

We also recommend you read *The Torch of the Testimony,* which recounts the awesome story of church life during the dark ages; and *Revolution* (vol. 1), which tells the story of the first twenty years of "church life" on the earth.

Our Mission, Letters to a Devastated Christian and *Preventing a Church Split* were published specifically for Christians who have gone through — or are about to go through — the trauma of a church split...a devastating experience virtually every Christian will go through *at least* once in his/her life. Because these three books (and *A Tale of Three Kings*) are virtually the only books written on this subject, you may wish to share these books with a friend who might need them.

Christian Books Publishing House sponsors a conference in New England each summer on the deeper Christian life.

Please write for further information.

BOOKS BY MADAME GUYON

EXPERIENCING THE DEPTHS OF JESUS CHRIST
Guyon's first and best known book. One of the most influential pieces of Christian literature ever penned on the deeper Christian life. Among the multitudes of people who have read this book and urged others to read it are: John Wesley, Adoniram Judson, Watchman Nee, Jesse Penn-Lewis, Zinzendorf, and the Quakers. A timeless piece of literature that has been on the "must read" list of Christians for 500 years.

FINAL STEPS IN CHRISTIAN MATURITY
This book could well be called volume two of EXPERIENCING THE DEPTHS OF JESUS CHRIST. Here is a look at the experiences a more advanced and faithful Christian might encounter in his/her walk with the Lord. Without question, next to EXPERIENCING THE DEPTHS, here is Mme. Jeanne Guyon's best book.

UNION WITH GOD
Written as a companion book to EXPERIENCING THE DEPTHS OF JESUS CHRIST, and includes 22 of her poems.

GENESIS

SONG OF SONGS
Jeanne Guyon wrote a commentary on the Bible; here are two of those books. SONG OF SONGS has been popular through the centuries and has greatly influenced several other well-known commentaires on the Song of Songs.

THE SPIRITUAL LETTERS OF MADAME GUYON
Here is spiritual counseling at its very best. There is a Christ-centeredness to Jeanne Guyon's counsel that is rarely, if ever, seen in Christian literature.

THE WAY OUT
A spiritual study of Exodus as seen from "the interior way."

THE BOOK OF JOB
Guyon looks at the life of Job from the view of the deeper Christian life.

CHRIST OUR REVELATION
A profound and spiritual look at the book of Revelation.

BOOKS by Gene Edwards

DIVINE ROMANCE
"How can I go about loving the Lord personally, intimately?" No book ever written will help more in answering this question for you. Not quite allegory, not quite parable, here is the most beautiful story on the love of God you have ever read. Beginning in eternity past, you will see your Lord unfold the only purpose for which He created all things. Plunging into time and space, you behold a breathtaking saga as He pursues His purpose, to have a bride! See His love story through His eyes. Be present at the crucifixion and resurrection as viewed from the heavenly realms. You will read the most glorious and powerful rendition of the crucifixion and resurrection ever described. The story reaches its climax at the end of the ages in a heart-stopping scene of the Lord at last taking His bride unto Himself. When you have finished this book, you will know the centrality of His love for you. A book that can set a flame in your heart to pour out your love upon Him.

A TALE OF THREE KINGS
A book beloved around the world. A dramatically told tale of Saul, David and Absalom, on the subject of brokenness. A book used in the healing of the lives of many Christians who have been devastated by church splits and by injuries suffered at the hands of other Christians.

OUR MISSION
A group of Christian young men in their early twenties met together for a weekend retreat to hear Gene Edwards speak. Unknown to them, they were about to pass through a catastrophic split. These messages were delivered to prepare those young men spiritually for the inevitable disaster facing them. Edwards presents the standard of the first century believers and how those believers walked when passing through similar crises. A remarkable statement on how a Christian is to conduct himself in times of strife, division and crisis. A book every Christian, every minister, every worker will need at one time or another in his life.

THE INWARD JOURNEY
A study in transformation, taking the reader through a journey from time's end to grasp the ways of God in suffering and the cross, and to bring an understanding to why He works the way He does.

LETTERS TO A DEVASTATED CHRISTIAN
Edwards writes a series of letters to a Christian devastated by the authoritarian movement, who has found himself on the edge of bitterness.

CHURCH LIFE
Gene Edwards challenges the lay Christian and minister alike to set aside many of the present day practices of the church and to respond to the growing host of believers who are seeking a living, vital experience of church life. The author calls for the laying down of some of Christendom's most cherished traditions and practices, telling the story of the origin of these traditions and showing that none of them have their roots in first century practice. He then proposes a totally new approach to church planting and church practice, so unique it can only be classified as revolutionary. **Church Life** should not be read by the faint-heared nor by those who are satisfied with the status quo.

PREVENTING A CHURCH SPLIT
This is a study in the anatomy of church splits, what causes them, their root causes, the results, and how to prevent them. A book every Christian will need someday. This book could save your spiritual life, and perhaps that of your fellowship.

CHURCH HISTORY:
These two books bring to bear a whole new perspective on church life.

REVOLUTION, THE STORY OF THE EARLY CHURCH , Vol. 1
This book tells, in a "you are there" approach, what it was like to be a Christian in the first century church, recounting the events from Pentecost to Antioch. By Gene Edwards.

THE TORCH OF THE TESTIMONY
John W. Kennedy tells the little known, almost forgotten, story of evangelical Christians during the dark ages.

CLASSICS ON THE DEEPER CHRISTIAN LIFE:
PRACTICING HIS PRESENCE
The monumental seventeenth century classic by Brother Lawrence, now in modern English. (One of the most read and recommended Christian books of the last 300 years).
The twentieth century missionary, Frank Laubach, while living in the Philippines, sought to put into practice Brother Lawrence's words. Included in this edition are excerpts from Frank Laubach's diary.

THE SPIRITUAL GUIDE
At the time Jeanne Guyon was teaching in the royal court of Louis XIV (in France), a man named Michael Molinos was leading a spiritual revival among the clergy and laymen of Rome! He actually lived in the Vatican, his influence reaching to all Italy and beyond. The great, near great, the unknown sought him out for spiritual counsel. He was the spiritual director of many of the illuminaries of the seventeenth century. He wrote THE SPIRITUAL GUIDE to meet the need of a growing hunger for spiritual direction. The book was, for a time, banned and condemned to be burned. The author was convicted and sentenced to a dungeon after one of the most sensational trials in European history.
Here, in modern English, is that remarkable book.

The following prices are for the year 1987 only; please write for our catalog for price update and for new releases.

Church Life (Edwards) ....8.95 hb
Preventing a Church Split (Edwards) ...8.95 hb
A Tale of Three Kings (Edwards) 5.95
The Divine Romance (Edwards).(10.95 hb) 6.95 pb
Experiencing the Depths of
    Jesus Christ (Guyon)....................5.95
The Inward Journey (Edwards) 5.95
Letters to a Devastated Christian
    (Edwards) 3.95
Our Mission (Edwards) 7.95
Revolution, Vol. I (Edwards) 5.95
Practicing His Presence (Lawrence).......5.95
Union with God (Guyon) 5.95
Final Steps in Christian Maturity (Guyon) ..6.95
The Spiritual Guide (Molinos).............5.95
Torch of the Testimony (Kennedy)..........6.95
Guyon's Commentaries:
    Genesis 5.95
    Exodus (The Way Out) 6.95
    Song of Songs 5.95
    Job 7.95
    Revelation (Christ Our Revelation) 7.95

Christian Books
Publishing House
P.O. Box 3368
Auburn, Maine 04210
207-783-4234
Visa-Mastercard accepted

These books are available through your local Christian bookstore.